THE NEGOTIATOR IN YOU

Joshua N. Weiss, Ph.D.

HRD PRESS, INC • AMHERST, MASSACHUSETTS

ISBN 978-1-61014-301-1

www.hrdpress.com

Designed in the United States of America

Interior Design by Christopher M. Zucker

First Edition

CONTENTS

PREFACE

THIS BOOK IS AN introduction to negotiation specifically for those of you who don't see yourselves as negotiators. Negotiation is a word we all know and yet we don't think it has much relevance to our lives. Negotiation is something other people do in a boardroom or at the peace table. And so you might believe it is not a big part of your life. Well, I would respectfully disagree. The reality is that everyone is a negotiator! We engage in many different kinds of negotiations everyday—with our spouses, parents, children, mortgage lenders, co-workers, or clients. Since negotiation is increasingly ubiquitous in our world you *must* understand the negotiator in you.

The Negotiator in You is designed to open your eyes to all the negotiations that are going on around you that perhaps you did not previously *see* as negotiations. From your dealings with credit card companies to conversations with your spouse about what to do with your finances: you are negotiating. Throughout this book you will come to understand the negotiation skills you *already* possess, how you can *improve* in places you struggle or are afraid to venture into, and how to approach negotiation in a *strategic* manner so that you gain a level of confidence that you currently may not possess.

In order to develop the negotiator in you, it is important to begin with a clear definition of negotiation and then analyze some fundamental concepts directly related to the concept and the process of negotiation. As you will come to understand there are a number of popular myths related to negotiation that must be debunked.

While most of us have heard the term negotiation, we can't really define it succinctly. Let's begin with a definition that provides us with a common jumping off point: *Negotiation is an interaction between two or more people who seek to meet their interests as best as possible by either reaching agreement or ending the process knowing they can do better elsewhere.* First you will notice that this definition is an interaction between two or more interconnected parties. Next we see that negotiation is about meeting one's interests (i.e. those things we need most in a given situation). Finally, note that the end goal is *either* the achievement of reaching an agreement *or* the realization that you can better meet your needs elsewhere. This last notion is critically important because many people define negotiation as simply reaching agreement. This definition puts significant pressure on the parties to simply reach agreement even if it is a poor one. So, the definition I propose is not your typical definition of negotiation, but these are fundamental components of negotiation to consider as we examine the negotiation process in more detail.

Next, we must debunk some popularly held myths related to negotiation. Many of these myths—perpetuated in the media and other public forums—give cursory attention to the art and science of negotiation. After explaining each myth, a more realistic picture of these concepts will be revealed.

MYTH ONE IS THAT NEGOTIATION IS SYNONYMOUS WITH COMPROMISE, MEANING THAT ONE SHOULD BE WILLING TO GIVE UP WHAT IS MOST IMPORTANT IN ORDER TO REACH AGREEMENT.

This is something we hear time and again in varied contexts and it is simply not true. The real problem with compromise is that it is frequently a quick fix solution to a difficult problem. As such, most compromises end up alleviating the stress of the situation, but do not maximize the potential value in a given negotiation situation. The reality is that successful negotiation, in many ways, is about creativity and coming up with unique solutions to complex challenges. Take the following scenario as an example:

Sarah, a representative for Dunning Contractors, was in the throes of a negotiation with Karen, a representative for the City of Cumberland. The negotiations regarded contracting services that Dunning would provide Cumberland as it revamped its reservoir. The two negotiators made good progress on many issues but were stuck on the difference between the amount the vendor (Dunning) was charging and the client (Cumberland) was willing to pay. This gap was approximately $100,000 on a $2,000,000 contract. After much back and forth, the negotiation was on the brink of collapse. Fear swept over both Sarah and Karen that all their hard work would go down the drain. At the last moment Karen said, "You know, let's just compromise here and split the difference. It won't be ideal for either of us, but something is better than nothing." After some hemming and hawing Sarah agreed, even though she struggled to figure out how she would explain this agreement to her boss.

What we have here is a classic compromise agreement that seems superficially quite fair given the circumstances, but ultimately stretches each party past their limits immediately putting stress on the two negotiators and their future relationship.

Let's imagine that we can rewind the clock for a moment and go back just before the compromise. We pick up the story once again to determine if another approach to the negotiation was possible.

As a reminder, the two parties are trying to come up with a solution to the $100,000 gap that has emerged. Instead of suggesting that a compromise is the best way to make this deal work—which is really not the case from either party's perspective—Sarah digs a little deeper.

Sarah tells Karen, "Okay, it seems like we have made very good progress thus far and we are left with this one issue. I just want to check with you, is there anything else that you and the City of Cumberland value that is not part of what we have discussed?" Karen thinks it over for a few moments and explains that there are two additional items that are important to her and the city that have not been included in the conversation.

The first is that Cumberland would prefer a multi-year contract to the one-year version on the table. Cumberland has taken on a new vendor each year. The costs associated with this revolving door of vendors are substantial in both time and resources. In addition, because of the turnover, Cumberland is getting a reputation for being hard to work with. With a multi-year contract that image will slowly dissipate.

The second is that Karen happens to be relatively new in her position negotiating these kinds of contracts, and she believes her lack of knowledge has contributed to that revolving door. This fact is unknown to the City Managers. Karen would also value Dunning's Project Manager teaching her the ins and outs of the work they will do so she will be better prepared in the future.

Sarah is quite encouraged by this new information because it also meets one of her core needs that until this point she did not think the City was interested in—namely a multi-year contract. Sarah was under the mistaken impression that because Cumberland had not previously done multi-year deals they would not do one in the future. As such, with the multi-year option she is able to close the gap in price by $80,000 because she knows that having the city's business over the long term is better for Dunning. In terms of the educational aspect that Karen desired, Sarah can give her that easily as it is a pretty standard part of Dunning's work. Sarah expresses her willingness and ability to meet Karen's interests. As a show of good faith, Karen agrees to make up the $20,000 shortfall.

Sarah and Karen reached a creative agreement because underlying and unspoken interests surfaced. Those interests held value for both and, in effect, made the agreement better for each party. That is the essence of effective negotiation.

MYTH TWO IS THAT THE BEST NEGOTIATORS ARE THE MOST EFFECTIVE ORATORS.

While being an eloquent communicator does not hurt, it is arguably not the most important skill a negotiator possesses. The reality, as the Danish proverb explains, is that you have two ears and one mouth for a reason. Listening is twice as important as speaking.

This is the case in negotiation because the currency of negotiation is information and the last time I checked, you do not gather a lot of information while talking. You do so when you listen carefully, which ultimately leads you to asking the right questions. These questions unlock previously closed doors and make a seemingly impossible negotiation situation much more solvable.

MYTH THREE IS THAT NEGOTIATION IS ABOUT REACHING AGREEMENT.

It may surprise you to know that negotiation is not necessarily about reaching agreement but rather that it is about meeting one's needs and objectives. Now, this may seem like a simple idea, but the problem in negotiation is that most people do not wear their goals and needs on their sleeves or they are sometimes unclear what those needs and goals actually are. There are different kinds of hidden motivations and information that one needs to uncover in order to solve difficult negotiations. Simply reaching an agreement, either a good or bad one, does not ensure negotiation success.

Ponder this example. Mary and Allen have been married a number of years. They have three children together and are happily married with the exception of one important issue: Mary hates how much Allen works. She knows he needs to work a lot to make ends meet but also realizes that for their marriage to succeed in the long term, he needs to spend more time with her and the kids. Mary explains to Allen that she thinks he is working too much and is worried about him. But she does not say more than that because Allen is always in a hurry to do things and has a short attention span. Allen hears Mary and decides that she must be right. So, the next day he calls some friends and plans a night out with them. The problem is that Mary did not tell Allen about all her interests and needs—his spending time with her and the kids. All Allen understood was that he should take more time off. While they did indeed reach agreement it was not a negotiation success because Mary's needs went unmet.

MYTH FOUR IS THAT NEGOTIATOR BEHAVIOR IS OFTEN UNPREDICTABLE AND PEOPLE FIND IT HARD TO DECIPHER THE OTHER NEGOTIATOR'S APPROACH.

The reality is that if you know what to look for in other negotiators, you will come to understand there is a universe of negotiation styles—five to be exact—that exist and not an infinite number of approaches. This concept becomes helpful because you can learn your own negotiation style, weighing the pros and cons of that approach and also learn to read another's style, considering how theirs might mesh with your own.

The following scenario illustrates this issue: Carl owns a company and Paul is his CEO. Carl has a negotiation style that can be best characterized as avoidance. Every time Paul raises an issue that is the slightest bit controversial, Carl becomes almost impossible to reach. Carl conjures up all kinds of reasons why he won't meet with Paul. Paul, on the other hand, has a competitive and assertive negotiation style. The more Carl avoids the situation the more Paul becomes angry and frustrated. Their negotiation ends with Paul quitting the company because he simply cannot work with Carl any longer. At the heart of their negotiation problem is their different negotiation styles.

With these important myths debunked, it is now possible to conclude this introduction with a little bit about the remainder of the book. This book is broken into three segments and can be read together or as stand-alone modules.

The first section of the book concerns workplace negotiations. The first two chapters in this workplace section address the broad topics of internal and external negotiations, their sequencing, the interplay between the two, and the role of facts and data in negotiations. Many specific types of negotiations the reader is likely to experience at work are found in these subsequent chapters, including: salary negotiations, negotiating with one's boss as well as in the virtual working world. Embedded in these scenarios are practical real world examples as well as various skills and tactics for handling a number of different, yet common, situations.

The second section delves into domestic issues. This section tackles the realm of people's lives where with they negotiate with family, including parents, grandparents, spouses, children, and the occasional nutty relative that everyone seems to have. From negotiations over drumsticks at holiday gatherings to the dreaded conversations about politics and religion, the different chapters in this section will help you examine how to negotiate at home, why it is different than other realms of your life, and provide you with some essential strategic tools to handle these negotiations.

Finally, the third segment of the book discusses various negotiations that you encounter as you weave your way through life. The various chapters in this section center on strategy and skills when trying to shift the other negotiator from a competitive to a cooperative negotiation approach; how to effectively assert for your needs; when you might make the first offer (or not); how to understand what value means in negotiation; things to consider when trying to buy big purchases such as cars and houses; and dealing with businesses as a consumer.

By the end of this book you will develop enough knowledge and skills to begin to become a successful negotiator in the different aspects of your life. But there is one catch—you have to use this knowledge and these skills or they will vanish as quickly as you learned them. You have to practice these skills, make mistakes with them, learn from those mistakes, and work with these skills to a point where they become second nature to you. Once you are at that point you will truly have begun to find the negotiator in you.

PART I

THE NEGOTIATOR IN YOU AT WORK

CHAPTER 1

INTRODUCTION

WORK IS A VENUE where you may well negotiate more than any other place in your life. These negotiations happen across the organizational spectrum and may include negotiations with your boss, coworkers, mailroom attendants, clients, vendors, subcontractors, and others. Why is it that we have to negotiate so much at work? One important answer to this question is that in today's world we are increasingly reliant on others to complete our work. As a quick example, take a moment and think of all the people you rely on to accomplish your tasks on the job. I am willing to wager that the list is much longer than you initially imagined.

If we are dependent on others to accomplish our work there are two fundamental approaches to getting them to do what we need or want. First, we can try to *tell* them what to do—particularly if they work for us and we have power over them. Second, when we do not have power over others or we choose not to exercise our power, we must resort to negotiation and persuasion to get the other party to do what *we* want them to do and is also in *their* interest. The second kind of interaction dominates most of our work relationships and therefore should be little wonder why negotiation is so ubiquitous in the working world.

Negotiation at work is very distinct and has its own unique dynamics that make it challenging in different ways than in other contexts. While it is impossible to list all the challenges in the work environment it is fair to say that the following are some key dynamics many people face when negotiating at work:

COMPETING JOB PERFORMANCE METRICS

We are all judged in different ways in our workplace. Our job performance is often gauged by certain metrics that indicate whether we are doing our job effectively or not. Yet it is not uncommon for some employee's job metrics to be in actual or perceived conflict with others in their organization.

THE STRUCTURE OF A COMPANY OR ORGANIZATION AND SUBSEQUENT SILOED DIVISIONS

Negotiations happen as frequently within a company as they do with outside entities. Interestingly, in most of the training sessions I conduct, participants usually remark that the most difficult negotiations they engage in are internal in nature. These often take place between employees and between employees and their supervisors. However, there are many negotiations that also transpire between departments within a company—such as between marketing and research and development. These are called siloed negotiations, which is defined as negotiations within divisions of a company that have to negotiate with each other to get their work done but largely operate on their own and have little interactions with each other outside of these negotiations. These negotiations are particularly challenging due to a number of factors. First, different disciplinary backgrounds create problems simply due to the way people come to see the world. Second, the lack of a common supervisor who can help establish the parameters of the negotiation adds to the challenge. And third, the lack of an understanding of the link between the different departments and the fact that that they all work for the same company and ultimately the same goal undermines the process.

VISIBLE AND INVISIBLE POWER ASYMMETRIES

Power is a dynamic that affects virtually all relationships in the workplace. While some relationships in the workplace have a clear power asymmetry—between a boss and their employees—others have what might be termed an invisible or shifting power relationship. The invisible power relationship is one that exists between, for example, two colleagues. It is invisible because the power relationship between equal employees ebbs and flows, shifting back and forth between them depending on the circumstances and varying levels of expertise on a given subject. So, in one instance, an employee might have power over their colleague as it relates to a technical matter. However, the situation might be reversed between the two employees when it comes to the ability to handle a relational issue.

DIFFERENT DISCIPLINES AND DIFFERENT AREAS OF EXPERTISE EQUAL DIFFERENT ASSUMPTIONS AND PERCEPTIONS

Different assumptions and perceptions wreak havoc on most negotiation processes. This is the case because these issues are largely hidden to us until uncovered by someone else and brought to our attention. However, the workplace context is particularly challenged by this problem because there are people in the same organization or company who come from different disciplines or distinct areas of expertise. These varied fields of study or expertise create a fertile ground for making assumptions and letting one's perception drive a process without either side realizing what is happening between them.

SEPARATION OF THE PERSONAL FROM THE PROFESSIONAL

The final dynamic that impacts the workplace context is the effort to separate the personal from the professional. In many workplace settings it is frowned upon to bring personal issues to the work environment. Yet that line is very difficult to hold and often ends up impacting workplace negotiations in subtle and covert ways. When someone involved in a workplace negotiation acts in what might appear to be irrational ways, the cause of that behavior can, at times, be traced to something happening in other aspects of their lives.

While all of those things serve as a backdrop to work negotiations, the focus for the rest of this section will begin with two broadly construed categories of negotiations that you will find yourself involved in at work. First, internal and external negotiations will be analyzed in some detail for their similarities and differences. Each is difficult in their own right and possesses unique challenges, but there is also an important interplay between the two that will be examined. Second, a problem that comes up frequently in workplace negotiations is a desire to focus on the facts. While this is a significant and often cited idea it ends up being very problematic in workplace negotiations.

The second half of this section of the book begins with a chapter about a negotiation we all go through at one time or another, namely salary negotiations. Then we move to a negotiation most of us dread but have to do from time to time: negotiating with one's boss. Then the final type of negotiation focuses on a completely different kind of challenge to the working world—negotiations that transpire virtually. This will include the dos and don'ts of negotiating with email.

CHAPTER 2

INTERNAL AND EXTERNAL NEGOTIATIONS: GETTING IT FROM ALL SIDES

INTERNAL NEGOTIATIONS ARE DEFINED as negotiations within a group, organization, or negotiating party, whereas external negotiations are with people on the "other side of the table"—such as clients, suppliers, or other countries or governments if we are talking about political negotiations. You might wonder why is this distinction important?

Before discussing the distinction between internal and external negotiations in detail you might be interested to know that many people report that internal negotiations, as a class of negotiation, are far more difficult than external negotiations. It should also be noted that external negotiations often have an internal element involved. For example, when one is negotiating with a client it is important to keep in mind that they are also negotiating with their team members about how best to approach the situation or with their negotiating boss on what they should be willing to accept and why. When this type of two-headed negotiation exists, the question of sequencing becomes very relevant. It is usually the best course of action to work out the internal negotiations first so that you can enter the external negotiation with confidence and consistency within one's organization.

That stated, when internal negotiations and external negotiations happen separately there are a few dynamics that are different and worth pointing out in more detail. The first variance is that internal negotiations tend to raise expectations in a unique manner. Most negotiators expect differences from the other negotiator in external negotiations. When it comes to internal negotiations however, many believe that these negotiations should be easier. After all, we're all on the same team aren't we? In reality, it is the closeness of working together in an organization or company that adds new layers of emotion to the situation. Sometimes this appears to give people inside an organization a license to say things to colleagues or coworkers that they would never say to their clients or other external counterparts.

The second dissimilarity is that internal negotiations are often required as a precursor to external negotiations. Unfortunately, it is not uncommon for people to mix up the sequencing and assume that they are all on the same page internally, only to find when they are in the negotiating room together that their colleagues have very different expectations, varying ideas on what they are willing to accept, and concessions they are willing to make.

The third distinction is that it is often fairly clear whom you are negotiating with externally. Internally, however, your negotiation process may impact stakeholders that you have not considered. Whatever the outcome of an internal negotiation, you are going to have to work closely with your colleagues over the long term so the consequences can be much more significant to you.

Finally, if you do not successfully negotiate internally the consequences of a lack of alignment can be that implementation does not proceed as planned or colleagues might try to undercut the process if they are not on board after the internal negotiation.

All of these differences suggest weighty problems when negotiating internally versus externally. The juxtaposition and the sequencing between these two connected negotiations are very important to pay attention to and carry out properly. Ordering negotiations incorrectly will almost certainly cause failure in at least one realm and probably both.

PERSONALIZATION WORKSHEET

Internal and external negotiations are a reality in most workplaces. The challenge of handing negotiations on both these fronts is significant because one process most often has an impact on the other. The following are some tips and questions to think about when preparing for internal and external negotiations.

START WITH THIS TIP: Check your expectations when it comes to internal negotiations. Internal negotiations are often difficult because we assume the other people in our organization should be on the same page with us and be working toward the same goal. If you temper your expectations and challenge important assumptions about internal negotiations, you will approach these processes differently, thereby reducing frustration.

WHEN IT COMES TO INTERNAL AND EXTERNAL NEGOTIATIONS, REMEMBER THESE KEY POINTS:

- Prepare for internal negotiations like you would any other negotiation.
- Internal negotiations include negotiations with co-workers/peers, supervisors, people who work for you, and people in other divisions of a company.
- When internal and external negotiations are required in a given situation, make sure to handle the internal negotiations first so you can negotiate with more confidence externally.
- Internal negotiations can be more complicated because it is not always clear with whom you will be negotiating, particularly when there are siloed divisions within an organization and you need to negotiate across these divisions.
- Remember that internal negotiations are essential for organizational alignment. If you do not have this alignment, do not negotiate externally.

QUESTIONS TO ASK YOURSELF:

- I am going to be negotiating externally. Do I need to engage in any internal negotiations to make certain I can negotiate with authority and clarity?
- In my internal negotiations, do I know the decision maker with whom I need to negotiate and their interests/needs?
- What are the dynamics that I should consider in my internal negotiations? And external negotiations?

- Will the process be clean, meaning that I can conduct the internal negotiation and then the external negotiation, or will I have to move back and forth between the two processes?

CHAPTER 3

WHY YOU CAN'T JUST
FOCUS ON "THE FACTS"

ONE OF THE BOOKS that I used in a graduate school statistics class was called *How to Lie with Statistics*. I really enjoyed that book and appreciated the honesty of the author, Darrell Huff, in highlighting the notion that statistics and facts can be used for many purposes. To this day I am constantly reminded of that issue in relation to negotiation. When people say "let's just stick to the facts" or "the data does not lie" be very careful. I call this the "just the facts" trap and it is important to understand its intricacies.

The crux of the issue is that there are facts and then there are facts that have been filtered through someone's perception then molded to fit an argument or perspective. What I mean is that two plus two is always four. We all know that and no one would dispute its veracity. However, what four actually *means* in a given negotiation context goes beyond a simple number to a number with meaning that is not neutral or benign.

In other words, some people in negotiation processes will take the facts as they understand them—which on the surface may be an objective thing they can observe—and apply their own meaning on top of them. This is where it gets complicated because the facts are no longer "just the facts." With subjectivity placed on top of facts they cease to become just facts and became an *interpretation* of facts that are *passed off* simply as facts. That is just a fallacious notion.

Consider the following example: I am negotiating with someone over the sale of a house and I have done my homework. I know that homes in the area are selling for a certain price, so I make an offer. The seller of the home says that his price is $50,000 higher than what I offered because this is what is common for homes across the country with the same specifications. So, in this case, he and I have chosen facts and data that are both valid and are in both our interests to highlight. I am using facts based on the neighborhood where he lives and he is using facts from a national level sample. They are facts to which we have added our own meaning and best suit our purposes.

In conclusion, how might you deal with this fact-based challenge? First, recognize that facts are not facts when they are filtered through a person's perception of the situation. These are facts plus interpretation. Second, the best way to manage this is to raise the issue with the other negotiator by explaining that you believe their meaning has superceded the facts. If they don't seem to understand, offer them an alternative interpretation or example.

PERSONALIZATION WORKSHEET

Detective Joe Friday, in the hit TV series *Dragnet*, was famous for saying "just the facts, ma'am" to women he would talk to during an investigation. While we try to do this in negotiation, we often can't focus on just the facts for a number of reasons.

START WITH THIS TIP: Facts cease to become purely facts when you lay your perspective and judgment over them. Yet most people don't make this distinction. Make sure to remind yourself and the other person of this reality. Remember this quote from Andrew Lang, "An unsophisticated forecaster uses statistics as a drunken man uses lamp-posts. . . for support rather than illumination."

WHEN IT COMES TO THE FACTS, REMEMBER THESE KEY POINTS:

- Which facts are we using in a given negotiation is a matter of choice and decision on the part of the negotiators—not some external, objective reality.

- Try to highlight the distinction between pure data and data with judgment for the other negotiator in a way that is easy for both of you to understand. Data with judgment is present when phrases such as: "I read the data this way," "From my perspective the data says this" and "The data speak for themselves."
- 2 + 2 = 4 is a factual statement. What 4 means in a particular negotiation and its impact is no longer a factual issue, but a matter of interpretation.
- Think of examples and precedents that the other can relate to when it comes to this issue.

QUESTIONS TO ASK YOURSELF:

- Which facts are being used in this negotiation?
- What other possible facts could be used and how do I make the case that these are more suitable for this particular negotiation?
- How can I raise the issue of facts with the other negotiator so we don't get stuck on this issue?
- What decision making process can we, as the negotiators, use to make the most fair decision about which facts are the best fit for this situation?

CHAPTER 4

SALARY NEGOTIATION: WHY THEY DON'T HOLD ALL THE CARDS

WHEN MOST PEOPLE THINK about salary negotiations they tend to take a very narrowly focused approach and hone in on the money. However, there can be a lot of other things people value in salary negotiations if you think past the money to what else you deem as having worth.

With this information in mind, there are a number of points to highlight when negotiating an employment contract. Let's begin with what I deem to be the most important. Many of us who negotiate our own salary contracts are often guided by a fear of consequences. As a result of this fear, benefits that are often available remain hidden because the average person does not ask for them. Most prospective employees say to themselves, "If I ask for too much the employer will tell me they don't want me working for them after all." That dramatic response almost never happens—so don't succumb to that urge. The reason you are sitting down to negotiate a contract is that the employer wants you for the job on some level. It is vital to go into this type of negotiation with a confident mindset because that will come across to the employer. If you do happen to ask for too much, they will tell you without simply folding up the proverbial tent and walking away.

As in most negotiations, preparation is the key to a successful salary negotiation. If you are not prepared, it will be apparent to the prospective employer and you find yourself feeling as if you need to take whatever the employer offers. Therefore, in the preparation phase, you want to make certain to focus on at least four important aspects of the negotiation.

First, think about your interests in the broadest possible terms. Ask yourself the question "What do I value most in this situation?" Many people stay fixated on money when, in fact, other things possess significant value. For example, imagine that you have two children and you and your spouse, who also has a full time job, share picking them up and dropping them off at day care. The day care facility is twenty minutes away from your prospective employer. On the days you are scheduled to drop off your children you are certain you will be late. Thus, coming in thirty minutes late on the days you have to drop your kids off in exchange for staying late or coming in early on the other days has value for you. In other words, think about flexible schedules, benefits (those you need and those you don't) and other interests you have that the employer could satisfy without giving up too much.

Second, don't rush to the money during the negotiation. Begin with other issues first, building rapport with your prospective employer before you get to the more sensitive subjects. Prospective employees often seem to want to rush to discuss the money to get that part of the negotiation over with. But it is important to remember that money is not all that a job is about. Certainly everyone has financial needs, but there are many other things to think about. Topics to discuss are: what it is like to work for the organization, how would they describe the organizational culture, is this a family-friendly work environment, what unique things do they do to build relationships within the organization, and what is the average length of employment? And don't worry—neither you nor the employer will forget about the monetary aspect of the negotiation. By discussing these other aspects of the negotiation first, you also send a signal that you have given a lot of thought to this job opportunity and you are looking for the right fit in a number of ways.

Third, it is important to have a gauge so that you know when you should and should not accept an offer. In other words, how will you know if the offer on the table is fair or whether you should ask for more? There are really two answers to these important questions that you should think through and research before the negotiation. The first is to understand your Best Alternative to a Negotiated Agreement (or BATNA, made famous by the book *Getting to Yes*) and the second is to look to independent or industry standards for assistance and justification.[1]

Your BATNA is the best alternative you have to walk away to if you do not reach agreement with the other party. So in the case of negotiating a contract, your BATNA could either be the unemployment line, another job offer, or something else. A lot depends on what you do or do not have on this front waiting for you outside this particular negotiation.

Next is understanding independent or industry standards. Sometimes a salary offer is not based on much substance and just happens to be what an employer would simply *like* to pay you. In other words, the offer has no real merit to it. When an offer such as this is made it is very important that you know what people in comparable positions are making and what the industry standard is for that position. Then, when the prospective employer tells you they only offer two weeks of vacation when you know the industry standard is four weeks, you have something to base your counter proposal on.

Fourth and finally, remember that this is hopefully the beginning of a long relationship so nobody—particularly you—wants to feel taken advantage of or mistreated. What this means is if you agree to something on the spot that you know is less than fair and reasonable based on industry standards you will spend the rest of the time at the company regretting it. And it is quite possible that it will remain a bone of contention.

To summarize then, remember that the most important thing is to ask, ask, and ask in a salary negotiation. When we don't ask it is because we often imagine that the consequences will be much worse than what they are in reality. It is essential that you push back against that fear. Also, remember that preparation is the key when it comes to the following:

Thinking broadly about what you value

Taking your time to get to the money issue by understanding other aspects of the organization

---

1 For more information, see Further Reading in Chapter 7.

Analyzing your BATNA and making certain you know the appropriate industry standards

Remembering that if you sacrifice what you really need, your new job will get off on the wrong foot and you will likely carry a grudge for some time.

Finally, let me leave you with an old adage that is posted on one of my colleague's doors. The adage states, "If you ask, and the other says no, you feel stupid for five minutes. If you never ask, you feel stupid for your whole life!"

PERSONALIZATION WORKSHEET

We all have to negotiate our salary at various points in our lives. You can avoid the situation and take what is offered to you *or* you can negotiate for what is fair and reasonable that best meets your interests. I suggest the latter.

START WITH THIS TIP: The word negotiation is part of the concept of salary negotiation. Don't be afraid to negotiate in this context. Remember the old adage "If you ask and the other says no, you feel stupid for five minutes, if you never ask, you feel stupid for your whole life!"

WHEN IT COMES TO SALARY NEGOTIATIONS, REMEMBER THESE KEY POINTS:

- Preparation is the key and is particularly important in salary negotiations.
- Make certain to find comparable examples to draw on from industry standards. This includes researching the salary of someone in a comparable position at a different organization. If this information is not readily available on the Internet, try speaking with friends in similar positions, understand their salary histories, and their rate of pay increases over time.
- Think more about your interests than just money—there are many spoils to be had in this context that won't cost your employer much, but will bring value to you.
- If you are in a difficult economic environment and asked to do

more work without a pay increase, ask for a schedule of pay increases in the future, and get it in writing. Or ask for other benefits that might not cost the company anything but reward you
for taking on more work (i.e. flexible schedule, telecommuting,
and so on).

- Talk yourself into asking for what you really want and deserve.
Once you have talked yourself into this, don't talk yourself out of
it.
- Think through your BATNA and theirs. Don't underestimate
yours and overestimate theirs—a common mistake that you can
test by discussing this with a colleague.

QUESTIONS TO ASK YOURSELF:

- How can I be persuasive to my current or future employer in this
context? How can I speak their language while still advocating
for myself?
- What other possible facts could be used in my situation and how
do I make the case that these facts, and this evidence, are more
suitable for this particular negotiation than other standards?
- What is my BATNA and is there any way that I can improve it?
And what is their BATNA?

CHAPTER 5

NEGOTIATING WITH YOUR BOSS: UPHILL BUT CLIMBABLE

AN ANALYSIS OF NEGOTIATIONS in the workplace would be incomplete if the subject of negotiating with one's boss was not broached. This is always an interesting type of negotiation to scrutinize because most people loathe this kind of challenge. Realistically speaking, however, we negotiate with our bosses all the time. And yes, most don't see the subjects one broaches with their boss as negotiating, because that is reserved for discussions about money, time off, or something that requires a formal sit down conversation.

To be fair there is definitely a unique art to negotiating with one's boss. If done poorly, there is always the potential consequence of ending up in the unemployment line. If done well, there could be an employee of the month plaque on your door! The following are some ideas to keep in mind when negotiating with one's boss about a raise, the feasibility of completing a project on time, or anything else you need to discuss with him or her.

Much of the success that ultimately happens in a negotiation is a result of the work done in the preparation phase of the process. This is particularly important when dealing with a power asymmetry, such as the one an employee faces negotiating with their boss. When preparing there are at least five things on which to focus.

First, know your interests and what really matters to you. It is hard to believe that people go into a negotiation unsure of what they really want but it happens all the time. When one clearly knows their interests—or the reasons why they are negotiating with their boss—there are usually multiple paths to a solution. Be firm on the end goal—meeting the stated interest—but flexible on how to satisfy them.

Second, look for supporting evidence or industry standards to make the case as to why the interest is justified. It is fine to say you want something, it is another thing to support your request with facts and other data that your boss will find persuasive. Negotiation is about persuasion and it is also about letting the other person have your way![2]

Third, think like your boss and understand his or her constraints. Too often people go into a negotiation without having considered what the other party is dealing with. This is not about agreeing with them, but simply about understanding their perspective so you use the right language to persuade them to give you what you are asking for. For example, if company policy is that a request for a pay increase must go through a certain multilayered process and cannot be approved by ones boss alone, think about how you might help them sell your request to *their* boss.

Fourth, recognize and analyze the power differential that exists between an employee and their boss. Bosses certainly have some power over their employees. No question about that, but what is questionable is where exactly does that power lie? A boss can take away a job in an instant and they could make an employee's work life difficult. Believe it or not, employees also have some power. For example, it is not so easy for a boss to fire an employee. There are lots of consequences. A boss would have to go through a search process, take time away from other tasks, and learn a new person's skill set and abilities. In other words, employees bring value to their organization and that is why they work there. That value translates into power to influence a situation. Try to remember that. Also, the power that a boss poses is usually perceived to be greater than it actually is in practice. So another part of dealing with power is managing the fear that power engenders.

Finally, after reviewing and preparing these first four things ask a co-worker, friend, or spouse to role-play the negotiation for a few minutes.

---

2   This paraphrased quote is attributed to Daniele Vare (Italian Diplomat), "Diplomacy is the art of letting someone have your way."

Try out saying what you want to say and ask the other person for feedback. Also, related to this, and especially if you are relatively new to the job, ask your co-workers what kind of a negotiator your boss is and what would be persuasive to him or her. The people who know best are the one's that have had to deal with him or her directly in the past.

Now, when you are actually in the throes of the negotiation process here are a few other things to keep in mind:

It is possible, and even probable, that some resistance to a request will emerge during the negotiation. Of course it is helpful to think through the places where resistance might come, but when one is in the midst of the negotiation and resistance emerges try as hard as you can to not respond in a defensive manner. One very good way to do that is to ask a question of your boss that garners more information about their resistance and also buys time to manage the emotional aspects of the situation. Furthermore, try to get underneath the resistance to their interests and why they may be saying no.

One's chances to succeed in a negotiation rise exponentially with their boss when they assert clearly and strongly for their interests. Assertiveness is different than aggression. Being assertive simply means standing up for one's stated interests and recognizing you have as much right to your interests and needs as your boss does. This is where most employees succumb during a negotiation. If one's natural tendency is to normally crumble under this weight don't make a decision on the spot you will regret later. Take any proposal that is less than optimal and ask for time to think about it. Then remind yourself that anything you agree to must meet your interests or you will be regretting it the minute you leave the table.

Finally, what would any negotiation with a more powerful party be without taking the time to understand one's BATNA or Best Alternative To A Negotiated Agreement. To understand a BATNA one needs to think very clearly about what they are prepared to do if they are not successful in the negotiation. Would you quit, go on strike, go over your bosses' head, get other employees to come with you in the future to meet with your boss? If you realize you have a viable alternative, you have now leveled the negotiating table to a large degree.

Negotiating with one's boss is an uphill challenge but it can be done effectively. Using the preparation tips and process guidelines should help to manage the peaks and valleys of this type of negotiation.

PERSONALIZATION WORKSHEET

Negotiating with your boss. Well, it is something we have to do from time to time so we can either embrace it or loathe it. When you loathe something it rarely turns out well. So let's go right to the heart of this kind of negotiation and see it as a challenge to overcome.

START WITH THIS TIP: Chances are that if you need to negotiate with your boss about something, it is an issue that is pretty important. Remind yourself of this reality and that it is quite likely that your boss needs you as much as you need them.

WHEN IT COMES TO NEGOTIATING WITH YOUR BOSS, REMEMBER THESE KEY POINTS:

- Remind yourself that you negotiate (informally) with your boss all the time. Think broadly about negotiation in this context because it will give you confidence that you can do this.
- Think of times when you have worked very effectively with your boss and how you did it. Pull out those things that were effective and use them in this scenario.
- You bring certain things to your organization, perhaps you perform certain tasks nobody does as well as you. Make sure to think about all those unique things you contribute to the organization and think creatively about how to weave them into the negotiation.
- Practice with a colleague, friend, or spouse and try out the things you want to say and for what you want to ask. Have your colleague, friend, or spouse play your boss and help you hone your messaging.

QUESTIONS TO ASK YOURSELF:

- How can I assert effectively for my needs in the face of a power asymmetry with my boss?
- Am I crystal clear about my interests, why those are so important (i.e. logic and reasoning), and how to frame them in the negotiation?
- What does my boss value in me and how can I use that to be persuasive to them? How can I use *their* words from the past to support my case?
- What source of power do I have in this context and how can I use it to help me in this negotiation?
- Are there constraints to what I am asking for that go beyond my boss' ability to satisfy? In other words, are there people s/he has to get approval? And, if so, can I help him/her to make the case to these other people?
- If my boss pushes my emotional buttons am I prepared for that and how best to manage that challenge?

CHAPTER 6

NEGOTIATING IN A VIRTUAL WORLD: THE DOS AND DON'TS AND THINGS TO CONSIDER WHEN NEGOTIATING VIRTUALLY

WE LIVE IN A brave new world—one that poses all kinds of challenges to how we work at vast distances. Since companies have gone global, the world has shrunk in many ways. This, in turn, has put us in all kinds of different and unique negotiating situations. New negotiations have emerged we never thought possible. Negotiations have become possible via basic means like email or more sophisticated vehicles such as video conferencing.

Negotiating through these virtual mediums is distinct from traditional face-to-face negotiations. The following are some dos and don'ts when negotiating in a virtual world.

THE DOS:

DO COME UP WITH SOME CLEAR GUIDELINES AROUND EMAIL USE. Email, is simply put, a poor form of communication in terms of quality of understanding. The general rule with email is that if it can be misunderstood, it will be. Starting a virtual negotiation with agreed upon guidelines on when email will be used and when it will be put aside to use other means, such as the telephone or video conferencing, is an important step in eliminating misunderstanding and managing expectations.

DO YOUR BEST TO MEET IN PERSON AT LEAST ONCE. Even though it might be difficult, it is really important to try to meet in person at least once in order to build personal rapport. The more personal time you have with the other the better off you will be. Think of it as an investment in your working relationship that will yield benefits over time.

DO LEARN ABOUT THE OTHER, THEIR BACKGROUND, AND WHAT IS IMPORTANT TO THEM. Take time to really understand the other, their working habits, their cultural norms, and what is most important to them. Experiment with some "norms" for email or other forms of virtual communication, such as beginning each interaction with a personal greeting or question.

DO RECOGNIZE HOW EMAIL AND OTHER VIRTUAL MEDIUMS CAN BE EMPOWERING AND GIVE CONFIDENCE TO NEGOTIATORS TO SAY WHAT THEY REALLY FEEL. People become more courageous when they are behind their computer screen and say and do things they never would in person. For accommodating personalities, this is a welcome opportunity. But don't go to far with this. A good rule to ask oneself is, would I say this in person to the other negotiator? If not, that is a good indicator to re-work the message until it is consistent with what one might normally do or say.

DO TAKE ADVANTAGE OF BUILT-IN TECHNOLOGY TO MANAGE THE EMOTIONAL ELEMENTS OF VIRTUAL NEGOTIATIONS. There are numerous ways of tempering one's emotions when negotiating virtually. Stepping away from the computer or saving a document as a draft to come back to when one is less passionate are good tools to take advantage of when the heat of the moment might be a bit too hot.

THE DON'TS

DON'T FALL PREY TO THE MISINTERPRETATION PROBLEMS THAT HAPPEN THROUGH EMAIL AND OTHER VIRTUAL TECHNOLOGIES. In the virtual world people make far more assumptions and negatively interpret another's message and intent in a way that they do not do with the spoken word or in a traditional letter. Given these phenomena, email should only to be used for basic conversations, to confirm one's understanding of discussions or agreements, or to summarize meetings. In other words, for very simple forms of communication. The moment a negotiation begins to get difficult with the use of email, cease using that medium and pick up the phone. Or find a more sophisticated means of communication to eliminate as many misunderstandings as possible.

DON'T FORGET THAT THERE ARE A LOT OF CULTURES AROUND THE WORLD THAT REALLY CAN'T WORK OR NEGOTIATE WITH YOU UNTIL THEY HAVE MET YOU IN PERSON AND COME TO TRUST YOU. Understand from the outset that negotiating with cultures that deeply value face-to-face interactions is exceedingly difficult in the virtual world. While one might be able to build some bonds via email, there will occasionally be the underlying suspicion that rears its head during difficult times in the negotiation, thereby throwing the whole process in doubt. A better strategy is to invest the time and money to go and meet people in person. After that, negotiations will become easier and when things get difficult you will be able to fall back on the fact that you have gotten to know each other personally.

DON'T SUCCUMB TO THE TENDENCY TO RESPOND TO AN EMAIL MESSAGE QUICKLY AND WITHOUT THOUGHT. It is very easy for virtual negotiations to "flame out" (i.e. escalate a situation quickly). This is most likely to happen when one reacts impulsively to what they read in an email. The key is not to react and respond immediately no matter what the scenario.

To sum up, negotiating virtually is an unavoidable part of the working landscape. If you know how to operate in this realm you can eliminate a lot of potential problems and succeed from a distance. But you have to recognize that this is a different world and requires distinctive thinking from a more traditional negotiation setting.

PERSONALIZATION WORKSHEET

Who would have thought, as little as fifteen years ago, that I could sit at my desk at home in the United States and negotiate with people from all around the world. What a blessing and a potential curse if you don't do it well. And there are a lot of pitfalls to be aware of!

START WITH THIS TIP: Simply put, the golden rule of virtual negotiations should be, if you would not say something in a face-to-face negotiation, don't write it in a virtual negotiation.

WHEN IT COMES VIRTUAL NEGOTIATIONS, REMEMBER THESE KEY POINTS:

- If something can be misinterpreted in a virtual negotiation, it will be, so expect it.
- Assume positive intention on the part of the other negotiator. If you get a potentially inflammatory email, respond with a clarifying question (i.e. a question that seeks more information or to clarify the intent of the other person). Try asking, "When you stated the following in your email what were you trying to say?"
- Take your time to respond to an email. Give yourself a break before hitting reply. And in the best case, ask a colleague to review the email for tone and other potential problems.
- Come up with clear guidelines together with the other negotiator about how you will use email in your negotiation. For example, some guidelines might be: 1. "We are only going to use email to summarize our conversations that will transpire over the telephone," 2. "We agree to check our assumptions and ask clarifying questions if we become angry or frustrated by what is said," 3. "We agree never to respond immediately and think carefully about how we frame our emails," 4. "We agree to use email in a more formal manner—such as the way we might write a letter."
- Avoid ambiguous words as much as possible and try to emphasize the emotional meaning behind what you are trying to convey because this often gets lost in virtual communication.

QUESTIONS TO ASK YOURSELF:

- What am I assuming and perceiving about the issues in the email or other communication? How can I check those assumptions and perceptions before replying?

- How can I try to build a relationship with the other person who I have to work with in a virtual manner? What gestures can I make to send a positive signal?
- How are our cultures impacting our virtual negotiations? Is there anything I can do about that issue? Is there someone I can consult about this challenge?
- Is it time to expend the resources to go and meet my counterpart in person? It will be costly in the short term, but pay off in the long term.

CHAPTER 7

CONCLUDING THOUGHTS
AND FURTHER READING

NEGOTIATING AT WORK IS fraught with challenges and pitfalls. Yet there are many common negotiation situations that can be handled well with some thought and preparation. Perhaps one of the biggest challenges exists in the mindset that we bring to the table and the preconceptions we make about what is and is not possible. "How on earth can I negotiate with my boss when they clearly hold power over me?" "If I ask for too much they will surely think I am greedy and not offer me the position!" These are real questions and fears that race through our heads as we negotiate at work. And yet there is no way around the fact that negotiating at work is simply part of the landscape. If one does not improve their skillset in this realm they are almost certain to be left behind as the working world continues to evolve or, worse yet, never reach their full potential because they don't possess the negotiation skills to succeed in today's world.

There are, of course, many other topics and subjects related to negotiation in the workplace not covered in the previous chapters. What you will find however is that the skills and tools mentioned throughout these chapters form the core of what you will need to know in order to negotiate in this sphere. As you manage your way through these negotiations you will notice similar patterns and issues that arise. Those become more and more manageable from a negotiation perspective the more you engage in these processes.

FURTHER READING

Lax, David and James K. Sebenius. *The Manager as Negotiator: Bargaining for Cooperation and Competitive Gain.* New York: Free Press, 1986.

Lax, David and James K. Sabenius. *3-D Negotiation: Powerful Tools to Change the Game in Your Most Important Deals.* Cambridge: Harvard Business School Press, 2006.

Fisher, Roger and William Ury. *Getting to YES: Negotiating Agreement Without Giving In.* New York: Penguin Books, 1981.

Mnookin, Robert H., Scott R. Peppet, and Andrew S. Tulumello. *Beyond Winning: Negotiating to Create Value in Deals and Disputes.* Harvard University Press, 2000.

Stone, Douglas, Bruce Patton, and Sheila Heen. *Difficult Conversations: How to Discuss What Matters Most.* New York: Penguin Books, 1999.

Thompson, Leigh. *The Heart and Mind of the Negotiator.* Upper Saddle River: Prentice Hall, 2004.

Watkins, Michael. *Harvard Business Essentials—Negotiation.* Cambridge: Harvard Business School Pres, 2006.

PART II

THE NEGOTIATOR IN YOU AT HOME

CHAPTER 8

INTRODUCTION

NEGOTIATING AT HOME IS something that we all engage in on a daily basis and yet many of us don't see it that way. Husbands and wives negotiate, parents negotiate—a lot—with their children, and we all negotiate at some point with our crazy uncle or aunt at the holidays or some other family event. Interestingly enough, at home is really where we begin to learn the skills associated with negotiation. As Jane Mersky Leder explains, "It is with our brothers and sisters that we learn to love, share, negotiate, start and end fights, hurt others, and save face. The basis of healthy (or unhealthy) connections in adulthood is cast during childhood."[3]

Now that we have, at least tangentially, established that negotiating at home is critical for a number of reasons, what is it that makes negotiating at home difficult? At least the following issues add to the challenging context of negotiations in the home.

First and perhaps foremost, we take for granted those closest to us. While most of us love our families very much we can often treat them worse than we would strangers. We don't do this consciously, we just know that family will always be there for us through thick and thin, as the saying goes. As such, we say and do things to those closest to us without thinking or we believe, in the end, that they will forgive us more

---

3 Leder, Jane Mersky. *Brothers and Sisters*. New York: St. Martin's Press, 1991.

than others will. This translates to the negotiation realm because negotiation requires careful thought and proper framing both of which seem to fall by the wayside when we are too comfortable. This is a generalization on some level but it is a dynamic found in negotiations at home and we must be very careful of this problem.

Second, negotiations at home are very different from negotiations at work or out in the world writ large, but many of us transfer approaches between these realms when the context is unique. At work, for example, we may be forced to make quick decisions under time pressure or to meet real deadlines. If that dynamic is something we constantly experience at work, we can bring these issues to negotiation at home when it is completely unnecessary. Or we become impatient with a negotiation process at home because it drags on without a solution and there is no forcing event to bring it to closure.

Third, and finally, while personality issues exist in the workplace and life in general, the close quarters at home can exacerbate this problem and add to the already long list of negotiation challenges. At work, for example, we might choose to avoid a colleague we have a personality issue with that we don't have to directly work with. Try doing that at home. It is not really possible and typically avoidance makes most negotiation situations worse.

The remainder of this section focuses on a number of varied negotiation situations that happen on the home front. The first chapter in this section looks at the impact of emotions in negotiation. While this issue happens in many different negotiation contexts as well, it is acutely important at home. The second chapter picks up another important negotiation challenge for families, namely generational negotiations. These negotiations are often rooted in hidden values that underpin people's perspectives. The next chapter delves into gender issues in negotiations, which are at the heart of many negotiations in this realm. The fourth chapter is related to generational and gender negotiations, but gets a bit more nuanced by concentrating on the intangible aspects that underlie many negotiations. The final two chapters in this section are the kinds of negotiations we face regularly, namely negotiating our way through the holidays and negotiating with our children—as youngsters and then as teenagers. Nothing like ending this section on an easy note!

CHAPTER 9

EMOTIONS IN NEGOTIATION:
HEY TAKE IT EASY BUDDY

SOMEONE ONCE TOLD ME, "Whatever you do make sure to keep emotions out of the negotiation process." I have come to learn this is some of the worst advice I have ever received. Why might I say that—seems logical enough! The problem is that negotiation is an endeavor that requires emotion and logic. One cannot simply cut out either element. To illustrate the point, imagine the opposite where someone says to you, "Hey, make sure to keep logic out of your negotiations!" How absurd would that be! So, if we cannot cut emotions out of the equation what do we do with them and how can we actually integrate them into the negotiation in a productive manner?

A more useful idea than trying to eliminate emotions is to think about how to manage the emotional aspects of negotiation effectively. You might be surprised to know that you can use your emotions to help you make certain points with passion and to highlight the importance of various issues in the negotiation. Thus far, we have been talking about this in the abstract. Contemplate the following scenario.

"Oh no," was the first thought that ran through Tom's mind, "Here we go again. I really hate this stuff!" Peering up from the folder she just slammed on the table, Amy let into a tirade on how their sole big investment in a Florida condominium project—an investment they both agreed to make based on

Tom's research—was floundering in the economic downturn and it was hemorrhaging money. From Amy's perspective it was all Tom's fault. Tom felt the blood rushing to his face as the hot-under-the-collar feeling he hated so much was back.

This time Tom was prepared. He took a deep breath, closed his eyes for a moment, and imagined himself on a cliff looking over a vast ocean. As the waves crashed, he felt the flushing in his face recede and the tense feeling slowly abate. He opened his eyes and was calm. "Amy," Tom began, "there is enough blame to go around. Whether we like it or not, we are in this together and we have both contributed to the problem. Let's roll up our sleeves and figure out how to manage this problem without accusing each other. Okay?" Amy, slightly stunned because Tom usually was the one doing the yelling, had never said anything along these lines before. Amy apologized for blaming Tom and losing control and got on to the business of trying to manage the problem.

What happened here is that Tom learned how to manage his emotions in the heat of the moment and changed a potentially destructive situation to the productive. How did he do it and how can you?

Before going into specifics, the best negotiators not only know a lot about their counterpart's interests, situation, and temperament, but they also spend a lot of time trying to understand themselves. This is particularly the case when it comes to the emotional aspects of a negotiation. Only after you know yourself can you hope to be persuasive and confident to the other negotiator. Here are some tips to assist you in the process of managing your emotions during negotiation—particularly when you are in a heightened state.

First, remember to step back and take a mental and physical time out. Don't react in the moment whatever you do. If you don't know what to say or are very emotional, don't say anything! As the adage goes, silence is golden. If you do say something in a heightened emotional state it is very likely to only make things worse or run counter to your interest. By taking a break you can put some distance between you and your emotions, thereby managing your reaction, and responding to the substance of the issue.

Second, know the things that are likely to set off your emotions. What are things that people say or do in a negotiation that really make you angry? Most of us know what they are so try to prepare for them. When they do come up, you will be prepared and you can step back and take your time to have your emotions without becoming them.

Third, make certain that your words match your actions. Nothing will show the other you can't handle your emotions more than an inconsistency between your nonverbal behavior (i.e. body posture, eye contact, etc.) and what you are stating verbally.

Fourth, think carefully not only about what to say, but also importantly, how to say it. If you are unsure in the moment, ask for a break to mull it over or to even call a friend. If you don't give as much thought to how to say something, as you do what to say, you will likely end up in further turmoil.

Fifth, so much of dealing with one's emotions is about managing expectations. It is best to go into your negotiations expecting some form of resistance when you express your emotional needs. If you take this approach with the right mindset you will be much more likely to handle the challenge this poses effectively. And you can always be pleasantly surprised if no issues arise.

Emotions can also be a direct result of stress and can affect one's ability to make prudent decisions and weigh risks in negotiation. Thus, think about managing your emotions as a way to handle stress and make the best decision as possible.

Finally, set up the process of working through a negotiation carefully. People typically have a forty-five to sixty-minute attention span in general, so develop an approach to the negotiation that has frequent breaks and keeps everyone fresh and engaged. If you have marathon sessions, emotions are likely to be heightened and people will be quicker to fall prey to their emotions and lose sight of what they are trying to achieve[4].

---

4 Mather, M. and N. R. Lighthall. "Risk and Reward are Processed Differently in Decision Making". *Current Directions in Psychological Science*, 21 (I): 36 DOI, 2002.

PERSONALIZATION WORKSHEET

Some of the early advice in negotiation was to keep emotions out of the process. But as we all have figured out by now, that advice is simply not possible to follow. Emotions are as much a part of the negotiation process as logic is and one would never think to leave logic out! The question then is how do you manage emotions in negotiations so you harness their power, yet not let them control you.

START WITH THIS TIP: Emotions are an indication of the importance of an issue in negotiation. When we experience emotions we need to recognize that the issue in question matters significantly to us. If we begin from this perspective, emotions are to be welcomed and will actually help us to find our way in a negotiation.

WHEN IT COMES TO EMOTIONS IN NEGOTIATIONS, REMEMBER THESE KEY POINTS:

- Have your emotions with control otherwise they will have you. To do this you need to recognize when your emotions are heightened, take a step back from the situation to get perspective and to listen to your emotions, and then engage the other when you are feeling more capable of having a challenging conversation.
- You do want to temporarily put some distance between yourself and your emotions in order to understand them and best manage them. This requires naming your emotions and examining how you are feeling and why you are feeling that way.
- When your emotions come to the forefront, have a technique to remind yourself this is happening and to deal with them effectively.
- When emotions are heightened, take a break or be silent, best of all, don't make any concessions because you will likely regret them later

QUESTIONS TO ASK YOURSELF:

- Why do I think my emotions are heightened? What exactly is pushing these to the forefront?
- What emotions am I experiencing and why? Is it something the

other negotiator is doing, am I just in a bad mood, or is this due to transference (i.e. is this a similar situation I previously experienced that did not turn out well)?

- As I go into this negotiation, what things are likely to make me emotional? How can I prepare to handle those?
- What technique will I use to make certain my emotions do not get the best of me?

CHAPTER 10

GENERATIONAL NEGOTIATIONS:
WHAT'S THAT SONNY?

IN 1990, A SCHOLAR named Raymond Cohen wrote a book called *Culture and Conflict in Egyptian Israeli Relations: A Dialogue of the Deaf* about the Israeli and Egyptian negotiation process at Camp David. The book chronicled how the process mirrored a dialogue of the deaf because the parties were talking past each other much of the time.[5] The same notion of a dialogue of the deaf can be applied to generational negotiations.

At times people from different generations actually appear as if they not only come from different generations, but perhaps different planets. When you do have a perspective that is clearly distinct and significantly varied from a person from another generation how do you try to manage that during a negotiation process?

A study by the University of Wisconsin indicates that the majority of generational negotiations and problems arise from value differences. The study says that understanding generational values and how these values developed can help people better manage and perform across generational boundaries.[6] There are a number of places where generational negotia-

5 Cohen, R. Culture and Conflict in Egyptian-Israeli Relations: A Dialogue of the Deaf. Indiana University Press, Indiana: 1990.

6 Benson, J. & Brown, M (2011). "Generational Differences at Work: Do they Matter?" *International Journal of Human Resource Management*, 22 (9), 1843-1865.

tions happen and where different values underlie the challenge. Here are some value based issues that cause dilemmas in negotiation.

First, Generation X (those in their 30s and 40s) and Y (those in their late teens and 20s) want a lot of feedback on who they are and how they are doing on a given task, but to them feedback is infused with a lot of positive reinforcement. Conversely, Baby Boomers (those in their 60s and 70s) are often more than willing to give feedback, but that usually means telling the other person all the things they are doing wrong.

Second, older generations define loyalty as staying in a job or relationship and sticking it out until they retire or perhaps their spouse passes away. However, younger generations define loyalty as giving 110 percent while they are engaged in a specific task, but when it is time to move on they are going to go.

Third, Generations X & Y have a specific perspective on respect. While they do value respect they just think it ought to be earned and in a way that resonates with the way they see the world. Baby Boomers often view respect as something that should be granted to people who are older and/or who have paid their dues.

Now that some of the competing values between the generations are clearer, what are some of the ways to bridge the gaps when you negotiate?

First, two way learning during generational negotiations is essential. Interestingly, people from different generations often feel the other should try to learn *their* generational norms. Despite their youth, Generations X & Y do have some skills that Baby Boomers can learn and vice versa. If Baby Boomers are open to learning a few new skills from their younger friends it is very likely the younger generations will be interested and willing to learn from Baby Boomers. In some ways this is also about respect.

Second, the good thing about values that underpin generational mindsets is that they are often not mutually exclusive. What I mean by this is that for me to satisfy the values that underpin my perspective they need not conflict with yours. There are many ways to honor and respect ones values without disrespecting another persons. In fact, because you approach tasks and value things differently there may be an opportunity for creative collaboration.

Third, try to think about the generational differences in the same way you might about cultural disparities. When viewed with this lens, it will help prevent one generation from thinking that the other should simply "do things my way." Analogously, if you are negotiating with someone from Japan you don't think "they should change their behavior to meet my needs." (And if you do, good luck with that perspective!) Instead you start from a place that recognizes that people in Japan simply do things differently than you. This is a good mindset to have in generational negotiations as well.

Speaking of generation disconnect, for those who do not know this, "brb" means *be right back*, "lol" means *laugh out loud*, "imho" means *In my humble opinion*.

PERSONALIZATION WORKSHEET

Generations come and go, generations overlap with many gaps in understanding. When this happens negotiation is necessary, but not always easy. What a generation values is different from another. Even how people in one generation act or see the world can differ from other generations. These are the challenges found in generational negotiations.

START WITH THIS TIP: Generational negotiations are most often about differing values that are usually viewed as conflicting or contradictory. That may or may not be the case. Most importantly, there is likely to be an aspect of respect in most generational negotiations. Try to look for respect and see how it manifests itself and impacts the situation.

WHEN IT COMES TO THE GENERATIONAL NEGOTIATIONS, REMEMBER THESE KEY POINTS:
- Look to the issue of respect as a central place where values differ from generation to generation.
- Think about intangible issues first in a generational negotiation. While it may be that the negotiation is over the use of a car, it is likely there is something going on beneath the surface.
- Try to put yourself in the shoes of the person from the other generation to understand the world in which they once or currently

live. Search your memory and experiences for clues as to how they see the world and everyone's role in it. For example, your grandparents grew up in a world that did not have computers for much of their life. That is hard to fathom for today's young people, but was a stark reality for those previous generations.

- Remind yourself of some current and past realities. Consider that your parents or grandparents probably spent much of their lives working for the same organization. This is a foreign concept for many younger people.

QUESTIONS TO ASK YOURSELF:

- Since I am part of a given generation, I am making some assumptions about this negotiation. What are they?
- How do I see important value related concepts, such as respect, and how does the other person see that idea? Are our perspectives necessarily incompatible? Is there some part of what they believe that resonates with me?
- What was the world like that they lived in and how is that vantage point influencing the negotiation?
- Is the main issue in our negotiation a tangible one or is it really about an intangible issue, such as dignity or respect?

GENDER AND NEGOTIATION: MARS AND VENUS AT THE TABLE

"When men and women agree, it is only in their conclusions; their reasons are always different."
—GEORGE SANTAYANA

Gender differences make their way into many realms of our lives and negotiation is certainly no exception. *How* gender matters in negotiation is an age-old question with some very interesting results that have been found. Many of those results will surprise you.

That stated, what can be revealed about gender and negotiation? One thing that can be stated is that there sure are a lot of myths and stereotypes when it comes to this topic. Men are tougher negotiators. Women are pushovers. Men would rather win than cooperate. Women need to act like men at the negotiation table to be effective. No, no, no, and no!

Another thing we can say is that beyond the real divergences between men and women is that the perceptions that men and women bring to the negotiating table are as important as any actual differences. Many studies have been done that have actually found very *few* disparities in how women and men negotiate. Exactly how those studies were done and the curious lack of evidence in and of itself is interesting.

To get to the heart of the matter, who better for a man to turn to in order to answer this question than a pair of women. In 2003, Linda Babcock and Sara Laschever published a book called *Women Don't Ask:*

Negotiation and the Gender Divide, in which they highlight the primary distinctions between male and female negotiators.[7] Please remember that these are generalizations and there are always many exceptions to the rules that follow. In addition, each of the elements listed below can be advantageous or detrimental in a negotiation depending on the circumstances. Finally, these points are framed from the perspective of what women do and are pitted, in contrast, to male negotiators. Here are the key differences.

Women are more likely to accept what's offered to them in a negotiation than men. Women don't ask for more because they are not expecting a give and take, but rather just a single offer.

From studies conducted with college students, the authors found that women tend to have lower expectations when going into a negotiation and therefore they are much more modest.

Women appear to not be as self-confident as men in many negotiation settings. When women do get the courage up to ask for something, they usually ask for less than men do and often concede more in order to reach a deal or preserve the relationship.

Both male and female negotiators make some of the above assumptions when negotiating with women. When this happens these negotiators take a tougher stance against a woman negotiator than they would against male negotiators.

Women have more of a tendency to be more relationship-oriented and cooperative. This can give them an advantage in situations where the parties recognize the value of the relationships and where a more collaborative negotiation environment exists. It can also cause women to shy away from raising issues that they perceive might harm the aforementioned relationships.

---

7   Babcock, L. and S. Laschever *Women Don't Ask: Negotiation and the Gender Divide* Princeton University Press. Princeton: 2003.

So, those are some of the key differences between men and women in negotiations. While male negotiators aren't quite from Mars and female negotiators aren't really from Venus, there are certainly some differences worth understanding.

PERSONALIZATION WORKSHEET

Gender and negotiation. There is little question that men and women negotiate differently. The real questions are how are men and women different negotiators due to gender and in what situations does gender impact a negotiation?

START WITH THIS TIP: Generally speaking, women tend to view negotiation in a much more relational manner, while men are more prone toward a transactional approach. This helps to explain why women hesitate to ask for more in a salary negotiation, while men don't seem to hold back from such requests.

WHEN IT COMES TO GENDER AND NEGOTIATIONS, REMEMBER THESE KEY POINTS:

- Gender impacts many negotiations in subtle ways. The context will be the determining factor as to how and in what ways.
- The perceptions and stereotypes that men and women bring to the negotiating table are as important as any other differences that may exist between them.
- Women tend to have lower expectations when going into a negotiation and therefore they are much more modest in their requests and approach. The reasons for this are numerous, but include negative stereotypes of women in power.

QUESTIONS TO ASK YOURSELF:

- Is gender an issue in this negotiation and how do I know that?
- What actual impact is gender having in this negotiation? Is it influencing the way I see and think about a problem?
- Do I negotiate differently with members of the opposite sex? And if so, do I negotiate that way all the time or can I identify certain contexts where my behavior changes?

- How have I seen gender influencing negotiations and what can I do to prepare for these types of negotiations?
- How does your approach change if you are a woman negotiating with another woman vs. negotiating with a man? And vice versa?
- Are you aware of the stereotypes about your gender when it comes to negotiation? How does that awareness impact your approach, if at all?

CHAPTER 11

NEGOTIATING INTANGIBLES: IT'S WHAT YOU CAN'T SEE THAT CAN HURT YOU

LET'S BEGIN THIS CHAPTER with a common family challenge. Take the story of John and his father, Aaron, who were at odds about a number of issues. Aaron was always after John for what he was doing with his life and the way he lived. Aaron felt John spent too much time carousing and not taking responsibility for much at all. Their relationship was strained to say the least and both knew it deep inside. And they took every tangible situation that came up—such as the use of the car or staying out past curfew—to negotiate the specific problem in question. They were ultimately able to solve each test, but the negotiations kept coming.

What is happening between Aaron and John from a negotiation perspective? The real negotiation problem is intangible[8] in nature as Aaron feels John should be more respectful simply because he is his father. Plain and simple. That is what Aaron did with his father and he expects the same from John. But this notion is completely lost on John and Aaron can't find the right way to raise the issue. Every time Aaron does bring the issue of respect up in the conversation it escalates into a full-blown argument. The intangible issue at the heart of the challenge remains buried.

Does this situation, or something very similar, sound familiar? It

---

8 Intangible issues are those issues that we literally cannot touch that make their way into a negotiation process. They most often take the form of a psychological dynamic, such as respect, dignity, or another challenges to our identity.

should because many of us have experienced times when a negotiation process has gone this route—with intangible issues at their heart—and we have been uncertain why that is the case. Of course, these intangibles happen in many realms, but are particularly important in negotiations at home with family. This last point is worth examining further because it is critical to understanding this issue.

In negotiations we have a tendency to focus on the substantive issues that confront us, for example, getting a project done on time, trying to work out an acceptable salary and benefits package, getting on the same page as our spouse regarding finances, or what we want to offer for that new house. However, negotiations are so much more than that because people are involved with all their idiosyncrasies. We bring to the table our tangible needs to get a negotiated agreement, but also our intangible needs of, for example, being respected during the process and preserving our reputation. These are the intangibles that often cause significant problems in negotiation when an agreement or some type of accommodation should be forthcoming. Therefore, how do we manage these intangibles during the negotiation process?

First, as negotiators we need to prepare and focus as much of our attention on the intangible issues as we do on the tangible. When we are working out how to approach a negotiation situation we need to remember concepts such as how to present our ideas with respect, for example, or how any proposal we come up with enables the other to save face.

Second, when we become stuck in a negotiation process, one of the things we want to do is step back and think about the intangible issues. Is it possible that the reason you are stuck does not have to do with the money or some other substantive issue, but rather that the other negotiator feels disrespected or that their dignity has been trampled upon? This is particularly important to remember when you are really having a hard time determining what the problem is between yourself and the other negotiator.

Third and finally, try to focus on something called the intent and impact problem in negotiation. The intent and impact problem is simply that we enter into negotiations with a certain intention and we take an action. After we take that action there is an impact on the other negotiator intended or not. This is really where the intangible elements can wreak havoc. As in the situation that was explained earlier, John was taking actions to live his life in a certain way and the impact on Aaron, his father, was one of disrespect to him and his family. Thus, it is worth exploring this issue with the other, explaining clearly that you are confused, what you meant by what you said in the negotiation, and trying to understand the impact on them. This will help you clarify the problem, if there is an intangible element involved, and to reach a mutually acceptable agreement.

To summarize, when it comes to the issue of intangibles in negotiation we need to remember to include these kinds of issues in our planning and preparation. In particular, think about intangible issues when you get stuck, especially when you can't figure out what the problem is. Finally, make certain to explore the issue of our intention with what we said and the impact it had on the other party.

PERSONALIZATION WORKSHEET

Often people think that life is about the tangible things you can touch, such as money. But the things in life that are most important are usually intangible concepts such as respect or dignity. These intangibles often matter much more in the long term than some tangible thing you might want to have in the here and now. Why should negotiation be any different?

START WITH THIS TIP: If you are stuck in a negotiation don't immediately think about the tangible issues that might be involved. Focus your energy on trying to get to the intangible or psychological issues as those are very likely what is causing the problem.

WHEN IT COMES TO INTANGIBLES IN NEGOTIATION, REMEMBER THESE KEY POINTS:

- When you prepare for a negotiation you need to focus as much of your attention on the intangible issues as you do on the tangible. Examples of intangible issues, also known as psychological needs, include: respect, dignity, identity, control over one's decisions and fate, and a feeling of belonging.

- It does not take much to trigger an intangible issue in a negotiation. Once these intangibles are involved, and have to be negotiated, they can be very difficult to deal with effectively. This is primarily the case because they usually become personal and sensitive to handle.
- Notice non-verbal clues and word choice. If these non-verbal clues do not match what is said, then it is likely an intangible issue is the underlying problem.
- Watch the intent and impact problem carefully, as many intangible issues can emerge as a result of this challenge.
- The good news about intangible problems is that the solution lies in the very same intangible realm. For example, if the other negotiator feels disrespected by your behavior and you want to solve the problem, you need to offer an apology and show them respect. While these are not psychologically easy to do, they do not cost you in the traditional sense of the word, and therefore are always within your ability to convey.

QUESTIONS TO ASK YOURSELF:

- Do I think there might be an intangible or psychological interest at the heart of the problem? If so, why?
- What clues has the other given that intangible issues may well be the real problem?
- Has the negotiation escalated quickly or become personal? If so, can I identify the intangible issues that might be the problem?
- What did the other party say or do in this negotiation and what impact did it have on me? Was the impact on me negative and one that touched an intangible challenge in me?

CHAPTER 12

NEGOTIATING THROUGH THE HOLIDAYS: JINGLE BELLS, TURKEY LEGS, AND FAMILY

AH THE HOLIDAYS. WE love them because we get time off. We hate them because of the crowds. We look forward to them because we get to spend time with family. We feel annoyed by them because we get to spend time with certain family members that drive us a bit crazy. All these scenarios and many others put us into negotiation situations that go well beyond turkey legs and where to put the mistletoe.

Here are a few tips for negotiating with your family and friends around the holiday table. To be certain, there are a lot of negotiations that happen during the holidays—particularly if you view negotiations in the informal sense. From what to make for dinner for the twenty in laws who are coming, to what to talk about around the dinner table, negotiations are everywhere.

Instead of talking about this in the abstract, here are a few typical individuals that might come to your home for the holidays and require skillful negotiations on your part. These folks might also fall into the difficult people category.

The first kind of person is the "know it all." We all have one of these in our family—some of us even have more than one! From how to solve the conflict in the Middle East to how to bake a fruitcake, this person has all the answers. In addition, they throw around obscure facts like "did you know yak's milk is pink?" Anyway you analyze it, these people are difficult and require a distinct set of negotiation skills to handle effectively.

How then do you handle the "know it all?" First, when they start in on the details and assertion of questionable "facts," pull yourself back to the big picture and remind yourself not to get into a tit-for-tat conversation. That is what the "know it all" wants. Instead, step back, don't say anything, and give yourself a chance to take a few deep breaths before responding. Otherwise the temptation to tell the "know it all" why they are wrong about everything they have said—which they often are—will be too great. Then try to think about their motivation. Often the "know it all" wants other people to know how smart they are. So here is a counterintuitive approach to try: let them be smart for the day. It does not cost you anything and it will make them feel important. After a while you may want to choose the exit option—available to everyone in any negotiation—and go get yourself some more Egg Nog!

The second kind of person we encounter during the holidays is the sensitive clam. At the whiff of any criticism or disagreement these folks immediately pull into their shell and refuse to come out for the rest of the holiday. You will often find them sitting off to the side or on the couch pretending to watch football when they could not tell the difference between a football and a golf ball.

And how might you pry open the sensitive clam? It is not easy, but the sensitive clam does not like to be embarrassed in any way, shape, or form. If they are embarrassed, or perceive to be, they will pull right into their shell. There are two tactics to try in this instance. The first is to get the person they have the best relationship with to go talk with them. The clam is very much a messenger person and if the right person talks to them in a calm setting it can bring them out of their shell. The second is to practice some empathy (or as the psychologist Carl Rodgers calls it, non-judgmentally entering their world) in order to get them to open up. By putting yourself in their shoes you might be able to comprehend why they have receded so drastically—not necessarily agree with their logic—but understand it. One useful approach, once you think you have an understanding of what is going on, is to ask them to talk in private. When you get them alone, ask them if there is anything wrong or that you are perceiving they are a bit withdrawn and wanted to see if everything was okay. If they are going to open up this will be the place to do it. If they say no, even though the contrary may be obvious, leave them and let them integrate slowly back to the group.

Before concluding this chapter, let me mention a few skills for handling the inevitable political or other sensitive issues that arise usually at the most inopportune time. People often avoid these conversations around the holiday negotiation table because they evolve into the same old positions and pointless bickering. That outcome is somewhat inevitable because we are usually in a debating mode with our families. A debating mode is where we try to find the holes in the other person's argument. Let me challenge you to try something different. Instead of responding by telling them how naïve they are or how moronic their last statement was, just take it in. Put yourself in learning mode and do the opposite of what the other expects. For example, imagine an emphatic uncle who needs to make his points fervently and with whom you always clash. Now conjure up the image of him saying something controversial and you looking him square in the eye and saying "Interesting point, I never thought of it that way. I'm not sure I agree, but let me think about it." Now imagine the look on his face—as the MasterCard commercial goes—priceless! He won't know what to do when you don't respond in kind and that will certainly alter the dynamic involved.

PERSONALIZATION WORKSHEET

Holidays bring many memories that stay with us for a lifetime. As kids we watch and listen to our parents prepare for, and manage their way through, the holidays. And it seems that every year, without fail, an issue comes up that requires negotiation: "Will we go to your family's house or mine this year?", "Who has to sit next to crazy aunt Judy this year?" You get the idea!

START WITH THIS TIP: Don't lose sight of the fact these are the holidays and whatever negotiations happen should not spoil the occasion for everyone.

WHEN IT COMES HOLIDAY NEGOTIATIONS, REMEMBER THESE KEY POINTS:

- Try doing the opposite of what your difficult guest might anticipate. This will really confuse them and they won't know how to respond.

- Many people who feel the need to assert too strongly for their interests often do so because people rarely listen to them. Think about just listening and hearing all they have to say without responding.
- Move yourself from a debating to a dialogue mode in which you try to learn from your guests instead of looking for the holes in their arguments. When in dialogue mode, you can learn something and also look carefully for places of agreement and disagreement.

QUESTIONS TO ASK YOURSELF:

- Why do I find this person so difficult to deal with? Is it just their personality or is it the context as well?
- Every year Uncle Charlie, Aunt Karen, or Cousin Dan says something offensive that pushes my buttons. How can I prepare myself to handle that constructively so I let them know what they are saying is unacceptable but does not ruin the holiday for me and everyone else?
- What negotiations are worth engaging in and why during this holiday? And which might I let go for a different time?
- How will you make the other feel valued and heard, while also disagreeing respectfully?

CHAPTER 13

NEGOTIATING WITH YOUR CHILDREN

"DAD, HOW ABOUT I help you with the lawn work and then you take me to the movies. How about $5 per week for my allowance? Okay how about $4? Dad, I really want to get earrings on my next birthday. All my friends have them!"

"Not until you are 13, honey."

"But dad!"

"You are right, that is unreasonable, how about when you are 12?"

This type of exchange is why I have saved the best for last when negotiating on the home front. Of course, that would be negotiating with your children. Negotiation starts very early on in the life of a child. In fact, negotiation almost seems to be a skill that children come to grasp pretty easily. Sure they have some issues with the emotional side of things, after all they are only a few years old, but they generally grasp the idea. And they do so sometimes quicker and are more effective negotiators than many adults. Of course, negotiating with children as they move their way through childhood and teenagerdom takes a variety of skills. Most importantly from a parent's perspective, you have to understand developmentally where your children are and what can and cannot be expected of them. In other words, you negotiate very differently with your five year old than with your fifteen year old.

The following is some general advice for negotiating with children. This will be followed by a few thoughts about negotiating during childhood (four- to ten-years-old) and then teenagerdom (eleven- to nineteen-years-old). This is something I have learned on the job with my three daughters.

In terms of general advice, first, children are more savvy negotiators today than they were years ago. This is primarily the case because the idea of negotiation has made its way into the school system and general lexicon much more frequently than in the past. Children are introduced to the skills associated with negotiation and put in contexts where they are using them more frequently.

While children learn negotiation from a number of sources, the most influential front are their parents. As a parent you are constantly on display for your children to watch, so how you handle your negotiations with them, your spouse, and the world around you is carefully noted and mimicked. Since imitation is the sincerest form of flattery, try to model the behavior you hope your children use in their negotiations.

There is an important line to draw with your children as a parent when it comes to negotiation. I believe strongly that negotiating with children in many different contexts is critical to their relational development. Negotiating with children has many positives. First, it gives them a voice in the decision making process. Second, it let's them feel heard, something most kids complain to their parents about. And third, it gets them using the skills of negotiation from an early age, something that will benefit them throughout their life. That said, the line I mentioned before has to do with when to negotiate with your children and when not to. Clearly there are times, for example, when a child's safety is at issue, and negotiation is not an option. Having clarity about those non-negotable scenarios in your mind and clearly communicating them to your children will help both of you.

Let me share with you a few specifics about negotiating with children and then a few on negotiating with teenagers. First and foremost, when negotiating with children you want to model the behavior you seek in them. The approach you take when you negotiate with them will tell them a lot about you. And the more consistent you are in your approach the better. If you do feel as though you are taking a different approach in one negotiation situation versus another, it is quite important to explain why you are making a change and the distinctions that caused you to make that choice.

When negotiating with children, it is very important to have clarity about any agreement you make with them. That means taking time to get to very specific details related to all the issues involved, including timeframe, checking their assumptions and understanding, and spelling out the clear consequences if they don't live up to their end of the bargain. Adults have the ability to read between the lines on various issues, but children are often not at that stage of development yet, they are simply too literal. Thus, the more clarity you can give them the more likely they are to follow through with the agreement.

Negotiation with children is as much about them taking responsibility for the things they agree to as it is anything else. Make certain, as your negotiated agreement begins to move into the implementation stage, that you hold them accountable. In particular, highlight the importance of taking responsibility for what they agreed to and explain that if they don't take responsibility it will be hard to trust them going forward. These are important life lessons as well as critical for their future negotiations.

When negotiations get challenging with your children use frequent time-outs to give you time to think about the best course of action. I will often say to my kids, "I don't think I should respond right now. Daddy needs some time to think through what we have talked about." I find when I do that, I am able to step back and come up with much better solutions than I would have on the spot. I notice I'm displaying a negotiation skill they will mimic in the future thus learning to manage the emotional side of negotiations.

Teenagers, as many who have them know, require an entirely different mindset and approach. My sister-in-law has a saying on a wall in her house: "Raising teens is like trying to nail Jell-o to a wall!" Ever tried that? Certainly not easy. And the most challenging times with teens can come when there is a disagreement that requires negotiation. As such, we are really at the heart of the most perplexing times that come with teenagerdom.

Teenager's number one complaint to their parents is that they don't feel heard. The first step is to listen and ask questions to try to understand their perspective. This is much easier said than done because being a teen is extremely hard for both parent and child. All kinds of things are happening to teens that they don't fully comprehend and these issues come out in many conversations in ways they don't intend, and don't really know how to manage effectively.

Know your hot button issues with your teen. As a parent it is critical to understand yourself first so you can manage your own emotions. You live with your teen every day and therefore have a good idea of what makes you angry and drives you crazy about their behavior. The question then becomes, what are you going to do about it if you know these hot buttons exist? Begin by reminding yourself of those hot buttons and when they are pushed, do not respond. Use silence as your friend. It is likely that whatever you say will only escalate the situation because many teens don't know how to manage their hot buttons.

Finally, name the issues between you and your teen directly and make sure to talk about intangible issues. For example, consider this story.

> Tom is sixteen. The last time his dad, Paul, let him use the car Tom and his friends put a scratch on the driver side door and left trash everywhere in the car. Tom did not say anything about it when he got home—gingerly putting the keys on the counter and going directly to bed. The next morning when he got in the car to go to work Paul found his car in this condition. Paul was fuming mad, but is also an avoider of these situations so never confronted Tom to discuss it. Instead he went to work and took his frustrations out on his colleagues. A week later, Tom casually asked his dad on his way out the door if he could use the car, fully expecting his dad to agree. Paul simply said no in a matter of fact way, turned, and went into his bedroom. Tom was angry and confused because he had made plans, but neither pursued things further.

What was going on this instance was not about the car, per se, but about Paul's feeling of disrespect. To negotiate their differences, one of them will have to name the issue between them and focus their energy on the lack of respect in question. In fact, most issues between teens and their parents in a negotiation are of the intangible nature so focus your energy there.

In summary, negotiating with your children can be a wonderful and daunting experience. Recognize that this will be a slow learning process, try to model behavior you seek in them, and when you are stuck, think to the intangible realm for answers.

PERSONALIZATION WORKSHEET

My four-and-a-half year old put on her shoes one day by herself. I noticed the left shoe was on the right foot and said, "Honey, your shoes are on the wrong feet." My daughter looked down, then up at me and said, "Very funny dad. I know these are my feet." Kids say the darndest things, particularly when you are negotiating with them.

START WITH THIS TIP: Kids want to be heard just like adults—maybe even more so. Even though you might feel like you know the answer to a certain question, listen to your child so they feel heard. That is what a lot of your negotiations are about with your children.

WHEN IT COMES TO NEGOTIATING WITH YOUR KIDS, REMEMBER THESE KEY POINTS:
- Kids are being introduced to negotiation earlier these days— give them credit and help them develop their skills.
- Kids mimic and model the behavior they witness. You can teach them to be effective negotiators simply through how you negotiate with them.
- Know the stage of development of your child and adjust your expectations to what is possible from them at that age.

QUESTIONS TO ASK YOURSELF:
- What are the non-negotiables that you have with your child/ teenager and why? Be prepared to draw this line clearly and explain why these are non-negotiables to your child/teenager.
- With a child's/teenager's desire to do more and make their own decisions there must also be responsibility. How will you make

sure that there is a strong element of responsibility and account-
ability in your negotiations with your kids/teens?

- How will you create clarity in your agreements with your child/
  teenager so there is no doubt about the consequences of not ful-
  filling their part of the agreement?
- How will you manage your hot buttons with your child/teenager
  and not let them get the better of you?

CHAPTER 14

CONCLUDING THOUGHTS
AND FURTHER READING

FROM THE PRECEDING CHAPTERS it is easy to understand the critical importance of negotiating at home. Beyond all the obvious reasons about the ability to manage your relationships effectively, the distinct aspects of our lives are clearly connected. And so what happens at home inevitably leads to impacting our work lives and other realms. But that is not why negotiating at home is so vital. Ultimately, without the ability to handle the myriad negotiation challenges at home we will struggle to have constructive relationships with those most important to us. This is something we will come to regret more as time wears on.

What is most interesting about negotiating at home is the multi-faceted types of negotiations we encounter. Negotiating with one's spouse takes one set of skills. And yet, negotiating with one's children requires an entirely different set of approaches. Finally, the other processes you engage in the middle of this spectrum necessitate another set of skills. In the end, negotiating at home presents a set of challenges perhaps not seen in the other realms of our lives because of the personal connection to every negotiation process. That personal connection—and the emotional elements—are at the core of our most difficult negotiations.

FURTHER READING

Brown, Scott. *How to Negotiate with Kids. . . Even if You Think You Shouldn't: 7 Essential Skills to End Conflict and Bring More Joy into Your Family.* New York: Viking Press, 2003.

Fisher, Roger and Daniel Shapiro. *Beyond Reason: Using Emotions as You Negotiate.* New York: Viking Press, 2005.

Fisher, Roger and William Ury. *Getting to YES: Negotiating Agreement Without Giving In.* New York: Penguin Books, 1981.

Kolb, Deborah M. and Judith Williams. *Everyday Negotiations: Navigating the Hidden Agendas in Bargaining.* San Francisco: Jossey Bass, 2003.

Kolb, Deborah M. and Judith Williams. *Everyday Negotiations: Navigating the Hidden Agendas in Bargaining.* San Francisco: Jossey Bass, 2003.

Peck, C. *How to Make Peace with Your Partner.* New York: Grand Central Publishing, 1995.

Rubin, J. and C. Rubin. *When Families Fight: How to Handle Conflict with Those You Love.* New York: Ballantine Books, 1990.

PART III

THE NEGOTIATOR IN YOU IN LIFE

CHAPTER 15

INTRODUCTION TO NEGOTIATION IN LIFE

THROUGHOUT OUR LIVES WE find ourselves negotiating for big ticket items such as a home or a car, with companies over discrepancies with bills or returning a product, or at the local market for clothes or antiques. Wherever we go in life, we are sure to find negotiation opportunities.

If negotiating in life means the negotiations we engage in beyond work and home, what makes this particular context unique? Here are some dynamics that are important to consider as we begin this analysis: First, the societal norm, at least in the United States, remains a competitive approach to negotiation. While there is little question many negotiations are being undertaken in a much more cooperative manner, one will still run into the competitive approach when they negotiate out in the wider world. Second, and in some ways connected to the first issue, we often do not understand how our reputation follows us around in life. The first casualty in a negotiation gone bad is one's reputation. And yet many people continue to be short sighted and go for the near-term gain, all the while sacrificing their reputation and the potential longer-term benefit. Third and again connected to the previous dynamics, most negotiations happen in the context of long-term relationships and are not one-time affairs. Even when we might think we have a one-time negotiation, such as buying a car, longer-term propositions are possible. For example, when one buys a car there is the long-term potential relationship between dealer and car owner when it comes to servicing the car into the future. This distinction is important because one will use a certain negotiation approach for one-time negotiation and a completely different approach when the relationship is ongoing.

Unlike the previous two realms of work and home, the kinds of negotiations one engages in during their life are significantly varied and challenging. All too often in this realm, we feel that we are in a weaker negotiating position and dealing with insurmountable odds. However, as you will see from the negotiation examples in this segment there is a lot that you can do to manage your way successfully through life's never ending challenges.

CHAPTER 16

GETTING THEM TO PLAY YOUR GAME: FROM COMPETITION TO COOPERATION

TO BEGIN THIS SECTION about negotiating in life let me take on a challenge I am frequently asked during the trainings and consulting I engage in with companies and organizations around the world. The question is often posed in the following manner: What if I want to take a cooperative approach to a negotiation but the other party is stuck in a competitive mindset?

As you might imagine, this is far from an easy question but there are certainly some actions you can take to try to help the other negotiator make this shift. The first action to take is to step back and ask yourself if a cooperative negotiation approach will best serve your purposes. Remember that a more cooperative approach makes sense in negotiations where there is very likely to be an on-going relationship with the other negotiator. This type of situation will happen most frequently in your negotiations in life. A competitive approach—where you try to get as much as possible for yourself with little regard for the impact on the other negotiator—is only appropriate in one-time negotiations such as over a house or a car. So, if you determine you do indeed want to take a cooperative approach here are some things to do to get the other to play your game.

Of course, in order to get them to shift from a competitive stance toward where you want them to be is to use the power of persuasion. There are many ways to do that, including trying to speak their language, but this is not going to be an easy sell. As such it is imperative to know your best alternative to a negotiated agreement or BATNA. In other words, what will your best course of action be if they will not change their approach and you are forced to walk away from the negotiation table. In instances where someone refuses to shift to a cooperative negotiation approach it is sometimes necessary to send a signal to them that either they take a cooperative approach or you will seek to satisfy your interests elsewhere. A hard message like this is often the only thing that will get through to someone who is being intransigent. It is very important to think about how best to frame this message, because it will almost certainly be received with some resistance. You should do your best not to convey your BATNA as a threat, but a simple matter of fact warning that these are the terms under which you are prepared to negotiate and that you would very much like to negotiate with them in this way.

Logically the next question is "That sounds like a good plan, but what if you do not have a good BATNA?" The answer is if you do not have a good BATNA, you should take steps to try to improve your BATNA. The good news is that BATNA is not static and can often be improved given time, creativity, and effort. Ponder the following example: I have a colleague who was helping a company a few years back. The company—we will call them Gizmo Inc.—made a product that required a very specific and unique micro chip that was made by another company—we will call them Unichip. After years of a fruitful relationship, one day Unichip contacted Gizmo and told them they were raising the price of their microchip. Gizmo met with Unichip to try to convince them not to do this because it was not fiscally sustainable for Gizmo, but Unichip did not believe Gizmo's projections and insisted. Gizmo panicked because Unichip had a monopoly on this particular chip and the increase would eventually prove to be unsustainable for Gizmo. This pricing shift might ultimately put Gizmo out of business.

It was at this point that they asked my friend to come in and help. My friend began by getting the story from them and then naturally asked what their BATNA was. They explained to him that this was exactly the problem and that they did not have any BATNAs. There were no other companies that made these chips. My friend engaged them in a brainstorming effort to try to improve their BATNA, which they begrudgingly did but with little hope of success. After a while someone said that there was a vacant plant nearby that was for sale and they thought the plant had been used in the past to develop some kind of micro chip. The team asked this person to investigate and he did. He came back the next day and said that there was indeed such a plant and it was for sale. It would not be cheap but they could buy the plant and see if they could get some retired people from Unichip who they were close with to train the people at Gizmo to make the chips themselves. The plan would indeed be costly but it was a better BATNA than they previously had and would allow them to stay in business.

With that new information in hand Gizmo asked for a new meeting with Unichip. Gizmo was able to persuade Unichip to come off of the price increase and take a more cooperative approach to the negotiation when they explained they had an alternative if Unichip insisted on going down this path.

To sum up, when it comes to trying to move someone from a competitive to a cooperative negotiation approach you should begin by revisiting your own approach and making certain what best serves your interests. Remember there will be situations (i.e. one time encounters) where it may not be in your interest to engage in a cooperative approach. However, once you have confirmed that you want to take a cooperative stance you may need to use your BATNA to let the other know how important it is to you to find cooperative way forward. If you happen to have a poor BATNA that will probably not be persuasive to the other, so try to be creative and improve your BATNA before proceeding.

PERSONALIZATION WORKSHEET

There are different games to be played in negotiation. One game to play is competitive and the other cooperative. In thinking about which to use in our life's negotiation it may be useful to turn to an authority on competition and cooperation, one Charles Darwin. As he stated, "In the long history of humankind (and animal kind, too) those who learned to collaborate and improvise most effectively have prevailed." Perhaps he was on to something as it relates to negotiation.

START WITH THIS TIP: You cannot change someone else's mind. You can only change the environment that they are in and help them to change their own mind.

WHEN IT COMES TO GETTING THEM TO PLAY YOUR GAME, REMEMBER THESE KEY POINTS:

- Use a cooperative approach when a long-term relationship is the pretext for the negotiation.
- The best tool at your disposal to get the other to play a more cooperative game is to use your Best Alternative To a Negotiated Agreement (BATNA) to send them a signal that you won't play their competitive game.
- If they will not play your game consider whether you should continue the negotiation in less than optimal conditions.

QUESTIONS TO ASK YOURSELF:

- Is a cooperative approach the best one for me given the context and situation in this negotiation? If so, why?
- If you do not have a good BATNA is there a way to improve it?
- What is their BATNA and how does it compare to yours?

CHAPTER 17

BEING ASSERTIVE IN NEGOTIATION: YOUR INALIENABLE RIGHT

AS THE CREATORS OF the Declaration of Independence wrote, "We hold these truths to be self-evident, that all men are created equal, that they are endowed by their Creator with certain inalienable rights, that among these are life, liberty and the pursuit of happiness." In negotiation, one inalienable right that most people do not fully embrace is asserting for what you need or want.[9] For without the ability to assert for one's needs and desires you will never be successful at negotiation. While this may sound rather obvious to some, this is a great challenge for many negotiators, particularly those who naturally tend to gravitate toward accommodation or avoidance. The following are some critical ideas to keep in mind when it comes to asserting for your interests.

First and foremost, you are just as entitled to meet your needs as the person across the table from you! People who struggle with assertion have somehow reached the erroneous conclusion that they are not entitled to the interests they have. Moreover, not only are they unable to satisfy their interests, but they should actually sacrifice these interests for the sake of the relationship. If you engage in this kind of behavior you will leave the negotiation table and deeply regret giving away what mat-

---

9 It is important to define assertion here so there is no confusion. According to the Merriam Webster's Dictionary, to assert means to speak or act in a manner that compels recognition, especially of one's rights.

tered most to you. Resist the urge and don't do it. The next few ideas will help you to do just that.

The second point to focus on is clarity of your interests, for without this lucidity you cannot effectively assert for your needs. It follows that if you do not have a well-defined idea of what matters to you most, you cannot assert for it in a convincing manner. I recall on a number of occasions being in negotiations with people and asking them what they needed most in a given situation. They fumbled around, hemming and hawing, not able to articulate what they simply had to have. There is nothing more ineffective in asserting for your needs than not being clear on what they are and why it is so important for you to meet them.

The third and final suggestion to remember when asserting for your needs is separating assertiveness, which is defined by Collins Dictionary as "confident and direct in claiming one's rights or putting forward one's views" from aggressiveness, which is defined as "inclined to behave in an actively hostile fashion." As you can understand from these definitions there is a very big difference between the two. Yet many people confuse the definitions fearing that if they assert for their needs this will be perceived by the other negotiator as being too aggressive. As a result they shy away from assertion altogether. So, in short, be assertive for your needs without the aggression; that is what the most effective negotiators do and understand the distinctions well.

In conclusion, asserting for your needs and wants in a negotiation is critical to your success. It is essential to remember that your inalienable right is that you are just as entitled to your needs as other negotiators. Once you firmly believe you possess the right to your interests then you have to explain precisely to the other negotiator what you want and why and not cross the line into becoming aggressive like others do.

PERSONALIZATION WORKSHEET

For many, being assertive in negotiation is a very difficult challenge. And yet being assertive is critical if one wants to be an effective negotiator because you have to be able to explain clearly to the other what you want and to do so with conviction. In order to be assertive one has to start with the belief that you are as entitled to what you want as the other negotiator.

START WITH THIS TIP: Being assertive starts and ends with one's mindset and should not be influenced by what the other negotiator does or says.

WHEN IT COMES TO BEING ASSERTIVE IN NEGOTIATIONS, REMEMBER THESE KEY POINTS:

- Assertiveness is defined as standing up for your needs without feeling the need to harm the other.
- Remind yourself of the importance of what you want and why. It is your right to what you want just like the other negotiator has a right to what they need.
- If you are prone to accommodation, and as a result waiver when you should be asserting, develop a technique to remind yourself not to stop asserting in the heat of the moment.

QUESTIONS TO ASK YOURSELF:

- Am I really clear about my interests and what I am trying to achieve in this given negotiation?
- Have I really convinced myself that I am genuinely entitled to my interests?
- Do I understand the distinction between assertive and aggressiveness? Do you know when you are crossing the line?

CHAPTER 18

MAKING THE FIRST OFFER:
SHOULD I OR SHOULDN'T I?

THERE IS AN AGE-OLD debate about whether a negotiator should make the first offer or resist doing so at all costs. Take the case of Peter. He was representing his firm in a negotiation with a new vendor over a large multimillion-dollar contract. Peter had done his homework and was very prepared for what was to come. When he sat down with his counterpart, Susan, he laid out many reasons why the two companies should work together. After a lengthy presentation, Peter made his proposal to Susan (in terms of dollars). Susan, leaned back, thought for ten seconds and said "That sounds fine. We accept your offer." Peter's jaw dropped momentarily, quickly recovering to offer his pen to sign the agreement. Peter had just fallen prey to the Winner's Curse. A term used to refer to a negotiator who has made an initial offer that has been accepted by the other negotiator without a counter proposal.[10] In other words, their initial offer was probably more attractive than it needed to be and so they won but presumably could have done better for themselves.

Contemplate the inverse situation, where neither negotiator is willing to put forth an initial offer. Jane and Tom have a strained relationship from a past interaction that did not work out well for either one of them.

---

10 For more on the Winner's Curse see Thaler, Richard H. "Anomalies: The Winner's Curse." *Journal of Economic Perspectives*, Year 2, Volume 1: 191–202. 1988.

Their trust is very low, but they continue to represent their respective companies with little hope of their relationship changing anytime soon. The contract they have been using the past three years has expired and they now need to negotiate a new deal. The economy has changed a great deal since the last contract so any precedent from the earlier agreement is not realistically appropriate. As a result of the mistrust between them and the changed circumstances, neither party wants to put forth the first offer—assuming the person putting forth the offer will try to deceive the other and the offer will be excessively high or low. Both negotiators hem, haw, avoid the issue altogether, and ultimately put an end to the negotiation. The distrust is too strong and the relationship ends in tatters.

These examples are slightly extreme, but they happen all the time around the question of first offers. From my perspective, the most important question is not which strategy to use all the time (i.e. make a first offer or do not make a first offer), but rather understanding the context because it is the latter issue that will help you decide if it is in your best interest to make the first offer or to worry about the issue of the first offer at all.

Given all of the information presented thus far, let me describe some contexts in which you might want to make the first offer and others in which you might want to refrain. One very important concept to remember is that the first offer question is one that comes up primarily in positional or solely distributive negotiations. What I mean by that is negotiations that are focused only on dividing the sum of money involved, and not those negotiations where there is a creative opportunity to enlarge the negotiating pie.

When then might you want to make the first offer? You may want to put forth the first offer when you want to *anchor* the negotiation.[11] What anchoring the negotiation means is that when you make the first offer the negotiation tends to get stuck (or anchored) around that offer and settles somewhere close to the original proposal. This can be done in both long-term and one time negotiations, but it is probably more of an effective strategy in one time negotiations because sometimes an anchored first offer can create a tension between the negotiators when one realizes what

---

11   This concept was first defined by Tversky and Kahneman in Tversky, A. & Kahneman, D. "Judgment under uncertainty: Heuristics and biases." *Science*, 185, 1974.

has happened. In addition, you may want to make the first offer if you have done your homework and have a strong sense of the potential precedents.

Let me give a few thoughts about what to do it you are on the receiving end of a first offer and how not to get anchored by it. To prevent becoming anchored by the other person's first offer, ask them questions about how they arrived at that figure and try to get at the underlying justifications. If they can give you logical explanations, make sure you understand what standard they are using if there are no other ways of looking at it. If they cannot give you a reasonable answer, it is very likely that their offer is artificially inflated. Both of these will require that you do some research beforehand and know the different standards upon which someone could base their offer. Furthermore, make sure to have a clear sense of what your offer is so that if you are asked for a different perspective, you can be ready to provide it.

Knowing the range where you want to settle helps you to make the first offer. Consider the following example. A colleague of mine called me a month or so ago and asked me a question about whether he should make a first offer to someone interested in a parcel of land his grandmother had left to him. This was most likely a one time negotiation and he had a strong sense of what the property around his land had sold for. My advice to him was to put forward the first offer as a way of anchoring the situation. Ultimately, it worked and he ended up in his preferred range.

When you might not want to make the first offer is when you are uncertain of what you really want in a negotiation or if you do not have all the information you need to make the best decision. If you are uncertain about your needs, putting out a first offer could be detrimental to you because the offer is not based on anything and hard to justify if the other begins to question you about the genesis of the offer. Similarly, if you do not have the information you need to make a good decision, sit back and let them make the offer and weigh the pros and cons. It may also be helpful to step away and take some time to process the new information before replying.

Finally, there are times when the first offer question should be thought of as irrelevant. For example, if one of your interests in a negotiation is to build a long-term relationship with the other party it should not matter who makes the first offer. If you are thinking long-term than the first offer in the initial negotiation is simply the first step in a long back and forth dance.

PERSONALIZATION WORKSHEET

Making the first offer in negotiation. This is a subject that gets a lot of discussion and everyone seems to have an opinion about it. The reality is that if you make a first offer, you should do it strategically and if you choose not to make a first offer, you should understand how to counteract the other negotiators initial proposal.

START WITH THIS TIP: Neither making the first offer or always making the first offer are the right approaches. Different negotiations require different rationale and logic when it comes to first offers.

WHEN IT COMES TO MAKING THE FIRST OFFER, REMEMBER THESE KEY POINTS:

- Do your homework and beware of the Winner's Curse, making an offer that is immediately accepted and was clearly too low.
- Don't get so entrenched in the idea of making a first offer (or not) that you won't make it at any cost.
- You should not make the first offer in a negotiation if you are unclear as to what you want.
- If the other makes the first offer don't get anchored. Ask questions and offer counter proposals that have merit and logic.

QUESTIONS TO ASK YOURSELF:

- Ask yourself if it will benefit you to try to anchor the negotiation with a first offer?
- Is this a one-time negotiation? If so, it probably makes sense to make the first offer to try to anchor the situation.
- On what are you basing your first offer? Do you have logic and rationale if asked by the other?

CHAPTER 19

VALUATION IN NEGOTIATION: YOUR MONEY OR YOUR LIFE

VALUATION IN NEGOTIATION IS an incredibly important topic for all negotiators to understand in significant detail. What is meant here by valuation? Simply put, valuation is defined as what a negotiator deems important to them in any given situation. That seems simple enough. The problem is that many negotiators focus the majority of their attention on one type of valuation, namely money. As a result, they completely miss or pass over discussing all of the other things that have value to them. This most often leads to inefficient agreements based on compromise or worse, a breakdown of a negotiation when a solution might have actually been possible.

As previously mentioned, often when we think of value in a negotiation we think of money. And that is certainly one critical element that people negotiate over. Money, however, is far from the only thing people value.

Take the following story as but one example: A few years ago there was a story in a newspaper about an elderly woman who recently sold her house. Not really news worthy, you might think, but it became news worthy for an interesting reason. The old woman, who was certainly not of significant financial means, sold her house for $25,000 less than what she could have received from another buyer. When asked by the reporter why she would give up $25,000, the old woman paused and stated, "Listen, I have lived in this house for 45 years. The person that offered me the higher figure told me he had plans to tear it down and build a bigger house. I didn't want that to happen so I sold it to a nice young couple that I knew would take good care of it!" From this example, we can see that the woman placed a significant value on someone taking care of the home she loved and wanted it preserved into the future.

When it comes to valuation here are a few things to think through: First, in any negotiation you must be very clear about the different things that you value, which can certainly include money but should not be limited to just that type of valuation.

Second, you must do the same assessment and investigation of the other negotiator and what they value. Determining what people value opens up new doors in a negotiation process and makes the impossible become possible—helping you bridge gaps when they exist. Conversely, a lack of an understanding of what the other values can make even the easiest of negotiations fail miserably.

Third, it is often common that people value different things in a negotiation process. If that is the case, negotiations actually have a better chance of being successful because trades can easily be made. However, to reiterate the point, for this to happen it is critical that these different values are understood or negotiators may miss the opportunity.

Finally, if you are stuck in a negotiation process and cannot understand why, it might be that you have not found what the other negotiator really values most. I had an instance years ago when an employee I worked with told me when I hired them that their salary did not matter much to them—what they really valued was working with me to gain practical experience. Later, after a number of issues arose, I came to understand that their salary did not matter in terms of finances, but it was important as an intangible sign of respect and an indicator of how much they were valued. Once I understood this perspective on valuation we were able to start a new negotiation process about the relationship and ultimately reached a more satisfactory solution for both of us.

PERSONALIZATION WORKSHEET

People value many things. In negotiation we often focus on the money as the source of value, but as we all know, money is not everything. People also value time, respect, and other intangibles that are a critical part of any negotiation process.

START WITH THIS TIP: If you are unable to find a solution to a negotiation and can't understand why, it is likely that you have not found what the other negotiator values. When you do, progress will be made.

WHEN IT COMES TO VALUATION IN NEGOTIATION, REMEMBER THESE KEY POINTS:

- Valuation comes in many forms. Try to find all the sources of value in a given situation.
- Finding common and uncommon places of value is how creative negotiation solutions are found and maximum value is attained.
- If you find that you and the other negotiator value different things, then your job becomes easier because trade-offs are possible.

QUESTIONS TO ASK YOURSELF:

- What do I value in this negotiation? Think broadly here about all the things that matter to you.
- Are some of things that I value intangibles, such as respect and equality?
- Do I know what the other negotiator values and if so, can I easily give them what they want and vice versa?

CHAPTER 20

NEGOTIATING BIG PURCHASES: I'LL TAKE THAT ONE, THAT ONE, AND THAT ONE

ANY CONVERSATION ABOUT NEGOTIATION in life would be incomplete if we did not include negotiating for big ticket items, such as houses or cars. While this is a negotiation that most people engage in at some point in their lives it is often their least favorite. This is primarily because of some of the dynamics found in these types of situations, which people tend to find uncomfortable. Furthermore, if you do not negotiate well there is a significant financial risk at stake that also makes people nervous.

The following are a few of the most common dynamics that I have found in these types of negotiations. After discussing each type of negotiation, a few ideas about how to manage them will be presented. The first dynamic involved in car or house negotiations is the type of negotiation approach most frequently used, which is a positional negotiation (also known as the high low method). To explain further, the positional negotiation approach is where a negotiator is concerned with getting as much of something they value as possible. In a car or house negotiation what they value is money. This approach is taken without significant regard for the other negotiator and what they are trying to achieve. Quite the contrary, as it is often rooted in trying to manipulate and deceive the other party. This type of negotiation creates significant distrust between the parties and is why most buyers don't like negotiating with car dealers or real estate agents. They find it very hard to determine if they are being taken advantage of or not. In fact, people disliked the process so much that car dealers and others tried to change this process and just put a no negotiation price tag on a car to take the hassle out of the experience. The problem, of course, is that that price was decided upon by the dealer and very likely favored their perspective.[12]

The next dynamic you tend to find in these kinds of negotiations is the good cop/bad cop tactic. Let's examine what this looks like in more detail using the example of buying a car. For those of you who don't know the process, the salesperson acts as the good guy, telling you he wants to put you in this car, and he will give you the best price, etc. When offers start to be made, the salesperson does not do the concession making rather he or she takes your offer and goes to talk to their boss about it. Their boss, the equivalent of the Wizard of Oz behind a curtain, is portrayed as the tough negotiator and bad guy who won't budge. In the end, the salesperson uses their boss as the bad guy to get on your side and make you feel as if they are working for you on some level. It has been an effective approach for a long time, but it carries with it the downside of the buyer ultimately finding out that they were taken advantage of and not returning to that dealer again.

The last common dynamic found in negotiations over cars or houses is the introduction of pressure tactics to get you to make a decision on the spot. For example, a salesperson might tell you this is the last car on the lot and if you don't take it someone else will (and there are others looking this is their last offer, or this is simply the best they can do. Or real estate agents might tell you there are other buyers bidding on this house and you will lose it if you are not careful. In short, artificial deadlines are floated in order to pressure you and to gauge your reaction. How can you tell if these deadlines are artificial or real? Probe the person putting these deadlines forth with questions—if some of the answers don't really make sense or the salesperson hesitates to answer them then it is likely these deadlines are conjured up.

Given these dynamics, how is it that you might prepare yourself to

---

12 It is important to say here that not all car dealers or real estate agents operate in this manner. In fact, I am increasingly hearing about dealers and agents who understand how their negotiation approach does not win them customers over the long term and are going to new lengths to change the way they do business.

negotiate over a car or a house so that you don't mind going through the process and you walk away feeling and knowing you got a good deal. Here are a few tips to use. First, as has been a theme throughout these chapters, negotiating over the price of a car or a house requires that you prepare, prepare, and then prepare some more. Knowledge is power in these situations and thanks to inventions, such as the Internet, you can do research easily and become an educated buyer. Go prepared with facts, figures, and a clear sense of what your bottom line is. In the past, this information was not available to buyers so the seller had a clear advantage. However, this is simply not the case today with such easy access to information.

Second, recognize the game the other is playing and do not play it— instead, work to change it. Tell the seller you have done your homework and you know exactly what you are willing to pay and why. If they try to negotiate you down from there, explain to them that you have already told them your bottom line and it is based on facts and you won't go below it. If they insist on doing the good guy/bad guy routine, let them, but just calmly repeat your message when they return. If you reach an impasse, don't be afraid to walk away. There are plenty of other cars or houses out there, particularly in a buyer's market. As an important aside, don't get yourself too emotionally attached to a certain car or house because that attachment will cause you to be susceptible to the pressures the other will try to impose on you. In the end you will forget about the research you have done to prepare and ultimately make a poor decision.

Third, ask yourself, "How would I know if I am getting a fair and reasonable deal for what is being offered?" This is a critical question and yet so few people ask it. You know you are getting a fair and reasonable deal if you know the value of the car or house you are interested in as determined by external measures like Kelly Blue Book and other websites. Make sure you understand the measure and why you are using this particular one instead of another. Equally importantly, understand that the dealer will also do this as well. So don't be afraid to ask them why the standard they are using is the best one compared to others.

Here is an example to consider: Imagine that you are in the market to buy a pre-owned (AKA: used) car and need to negotiate the price with a dealer. Because you have read this book you think to yourself, I need to be prepared! And so you start doing some research on the web, thinking to yourself that it would be good to have an external standard to make your case. Being the educated consumer that you are you go to the Kelley Blue Book Value website, famous for providing data on how much you should pay for a car. With all this information in hand, as well as what you can afford to pay, you head down to the dealer and make a deal. After visiting a few dealers to get the best price you land on a deal that is better than the blue book value by $1,000. Not a bad deal you think to yourself and you walk away a happy consumer!

What is wrong with this picture? The external standard you used is not actually the best standard you could have used. While the Kelley Blue Book does tell you what a car is worth, it does not tell you what the dealer actually paid for the car. In all honesty, that is the real figure that you need to know in order to make the best deal possible. Those figures, what a dealer would expect to pay wholesale for a car, can be had at a website called www.galves.com. That information is right there out on the web for anyone to find, but very few people do because it is one of the best kept secrets out there.

Lastly, the real key to tipping a car or house negotiation to your advantage is a clear understanding of your alternatives. For example, when going car shopping my strong suggestion is to find a car dealer who is lined up along a highway where there are many other dealers. Why would I say that? Well, imagine that you go to such a dealer and you feel like they are really squeezing you and pressuring you in a very uncomfortable manner. What do you have at your disposal? If you get up and leave, walking next door to the dealer's competitor, you have a great alternative. And you can do some comparison shopping at the second dealer to see how their prices compares to the first. In fact, it is not bad to go to a few dealers to compare. If a dealer gives you a take it or leave it offer and you come back later they will most often give you the proposed deal.

PERSONALIZATION WORKSHEET

To make big purchases in life we usually have to negotiate. The kind of negotiation that happens around this type of transaction is often uncomfortable for a lot of people. We can play a positional game of negotiation well and still be consistent with our values.

START WITH THIS TIP: Expect a positional, high-low negotiation and play the game the right way. Prepare so that you ultimately know where you want to land in this negotiation and adjust your concessions as needed. Understanding where you want to end up will help you to make the difficult decisions in this kind of negotiation.

WHEN IT COMES NEGOTIATIONS AROUND BIG PURCHASES, REMEMBER THESE KEY POINTS:

- Doing your homework and preparing for these kinds of negotiations is critical to your success. In this case, information is power and the Internet has leveled the playing field between buyer and seller.
- Make sure you investigate all the standards used in these kinds of negotiations (i.e. for cars, Kelly Blue Book and Galves). While it is fine for the other person to use a certain standard there are other standards out there that might better fit your perspective and you should not hesitate to raise those and actually negotiate the standards to be used.
- Watch the good cop/bad cop approach that many sellers use in negotiations. Let them go through their routine while you keep your goal in mind. As long as you end up where you want to it does not matter what games the other side plays.

QUESTIONS TO ASK YOURSELF:

- What do I want to pay for this item and how can I justify my price? What criteria will I use to support my perspective?
- What standards are out there for me to find when it comes to buying a house or a car? And which one is best for me given the context of this negotiation?
- How will I handle pressure tactics, the use of deadlines, and other tricks so that I don't become susceptible to them?

CHAPTER 21

NEGOTIATING WITH COMPANIES AS THE WEAK CONSUMER: THEY HUFF AND THEY PUFF

NEGOTIATING WITH COMPANIES CAN often feel like negotiating with the big bad wolf. You, as the consumer, can feel like one of the three little pigs trapped in the house waiting to see if it will get blown down and if you'll be eaten. Probably not the image companies would want to give you, but as the consumer you are sometimes treated or feel this way. Certainly companies do go out of their way to say the "customer is king" or the "customer is always right," that is until a problem comes up. Then things change a bit and when you call to negotiate, you might hear canned phrases like "I am sorry but that is our policy" or some other rigid approach to the problem you are raising. Suffice it to say you are the weaker party in that context. How might you then negotiate with a more powerful counterpart? In general, dealing with power in a negotiation is indeed a challenge, but there are many stories of weaker parties doing well in meeting their interests in these difficult negotiations.

To that end, I am reminded of a story from the international realm that is instructive for this purpose. Way back in 1964, a number of smaller developing nations in the world were being taken advantage of, and even excluded from various negotiation processes, when it came to economic decisions that were impacting the global system and their own countries. Many of these nations got together and asked each other what they could do to get their voice heard and improve their negotiating power with the larger, more powerful nations. The answer was the formation of the G-77 (Group of 77). As the largest Third World coalition in the United Nations, the G-77 provides the means for the developing world to articulate and promote its collective economic interests and enhance its joint negotiating capacity on all major international economic issues, while also promoting economic and technical cooperation among developing countries. What this story is really about is the search for power when entities don't have any. These nations took a creative approach to enhance their power and so can you when faced with a similar daunting challenge.

This story also points to the first way to try to improve your power as a weaker party, namely to build coalitions and find allies who have the same goals and interests. This not only happens at the international level, but also in the organizational realm and in society in general. For example, I was recently teaching a class where a woman told me about a boss that she had that was really difficult to get along with. However, it was unlikely that he could be fired given he belonged to a strong union. As she put it, "There is nothing I can do." I asked her, "Do other people in your department feel this way? If so, how many would you say?" She thought about it for a moment and said, "Yes others feel this way and there are ten people (including me) in my department—all of whom feel our boss is very difficult to work with and would like to see him change his ways." We initially talked about her going to meet her boss by herself to negotiate, but she thought that would lead nowhere. As she explained, "If I threatened to quit he would probably let me, to look tough." I then asked, "What would the negotiation look like if you and the other nine people in the department went to him and explained that unless he changed his approach to management you would all quit en masse." She laughed and stated, "That would certainly get his attention in a way that no one of us could individually." But then a light bulb went off and she decided it was a good idea and worth a try. She reported back to me later that they did this and he quit a month later over pressure to change his management style. Thus, one way to handle power when you are the weaker party is to build coalitions and find allies with the same interests as you. This of course is also possible to do in the context of dealing with companies. As a consumer you can connect with consumer advocacy groups, such as the Better Business Bureau, to help influence the situation.

The second thing to try when negotiating with a more powerful party is to make certain you are clear about your and their alternatives or what action you will take if you cannot reach agreement. When you examine both your and their alternatives you can determine just how powerful the other party is exactly and also analyze the consequences of exercising your alternative away from the table. Also, remember that even if they have a good alternative they may be hesitant to use it. There are consequences for the more powerful party as well. If a company gains a reputation for treating customers poorly that has significant consequences for them in the long-term.

The third approach to negotiating with a stronger party is to remember that power is actually a relational concept. What this means is that people only hold power over others if one values what the other has. For example, if you have the ability to pay me a lot of money to do a job, but not meet my core interest of a flexible schedule so I can spend more time with my kids, you do not hold as much power over me as if I valued money first and foremost. The moment the other party sits down with you they are recognizing you have influence in the situation and that translates into power for you. If they could simply impose their will on you they would do that. But they cannot, which is why you are sitting with them. It is vital to remind yourself of this fact, which also should be empowering for you as you sit down to negotiate.

The final way that a weaker party in a negotiation can deal with a more powerful party is to send a message that you do not perceive yourself to be weaker. Because power is an ambiguous concept it is easy to cast doubt even on the most powerful of people. Take the following story as an example. An employee, with a special technical expertise, heard rumors she was to be fired from their job given the downturn in the economy. As she thought about it initially, there was not much she could do. Later that day her boss called and asked to see her in an hour. During that hour the employee thought hard about this predicament and realized that she was the only one who could provide a specific expertise for the company. She started to build the case that if the company were to subcontract this work out it would cost more than keeping her as an employee. When she met with her boss, she came with all this information and was able to make a persuasive case to keep her on. Her boss did so.

In summary, if you are the weaker party in a negotiation try to build coalitions and alliances, clearly understand your and their alternatives—what you can do away from the table, realize that power is a relational concept and the other may not hold power over you in the way you think, and finally, send a message to the more powerful party that even if they hold most of the cards you still have an ability to influence the situation in various ways.

PERSONALIZATION WORKSHEET

Many big companies nowadays believe that the consumer is king, until a problem arises. Then the customer as king becomes subject to policies and other rules the company has made up so they don't need to negotiate. This frustrates the consumer to the point where they simply give up or give in.

START WITH THIS TIP: If you view yourself as the weak consumer without any options at your disposal that is what you will become. Think of yourself as someone with options and be creative about how to approach your negotiations. If you take a creative and alternate approach the company is not expecting it will pay dividends.

WHEN IT COMES TO NEGOTIATING WITH BIG COMPANIES, REMEMBER THESE KEY POINTS:

- You have options—find them.
- Rules and policies that a company has are not written in stone. Challenge the veracity of the rules or policies if they do not make sense or seem unfair.
- If you speak to a customer service representative and are getting nowhere don't be afraid to ask to speak to a supervisor. Often customer service representatives are given strict rules to follow while their supervisors have more leeway to be creative.
- Do some homework and investigate the company policy with regard to the issue in question.

QUESTIONS TO ASK YOURSELF:

- What do I want from this negotiation? Am I clear about what is wrong and what I am asking them to do?
- How can I improve my BATNA in this situation? Is there an advocacy group that can help me to level the playing field?
- What power does the company hold over me and is there a way of creatively challenging that?
- How can I convey to the company that I hold some power in this negotiation and unless my claim is taken seriously, I will consider exercising that power?

CHAPTER 22

CONCLUDING THOUGHTS AND FURTHER READING

AS THE READER CAN understand from the breadth of subjects covered in the preceding chapters, negotiating in life can take numerous forms and present many trials. This area is clearly distinct from negotiating at work and at home where negotiations are likely to be personal and long-term in nature. So it is fair to argue that negotiations in life pose unique tests for our ability to negotiate and forces us to manage an entirely different set of problems.

Much of our negotiations in life are subject to dynamics outside of our control that significantly impact our approach. For example, negotiating for a house requires a spectrum of skills depending on the economic conditions at the time. If we are seeking a home in a buyer's market we might find ourselves in a more powerful position and therefore can more easily control the process. The opposite is true if we are in a seller's market—making our preparation that much more critical so we can make a decisive offer quickly.

Or as another example, if we are forced to negotiate with a company over the return of a product or to dispute a credit card bill, we usually feel as though we come to the table from a position of weakness. As such, we must be creative and persistent, using many tools at our disposal if we know they are there. These various fluctuations in the negotiating context, and subsequently our negotiating positions, make negotiating in life an adventure that is full of surprises.

Intangible concepts that we discussed in previous chapters also take negotiations in life to another level of difficulty. Hidden aspects such as what people value and what kind of negotiation approach the other negotiator is using (competitive or cooperative) keep us guessing. Moreover, the stresses of issues at home and at work can carry over into negotiations in life. If one is having a bad day at work and then has to negotiate over a problem with their credit card company, it is likely that the customer service representative will suffer the impact of those frustrations during the negotiation process.

Finally, the importance of being able to negotiate in life and navigate our way through the endless tests life puts in front of us should not be underestimated. I recall a comment one of my former students made ten years ago that is still vivid for me and was really the impetus for this book. I was teaching an adult education course on negotiation and dispute resolution at a small women's college in Western Massachusetts. At the end of the semester a woman in her late sixties came up to me and said, "You know, if I had learned these skills thirty years ago, my life would have been very different. I think of all the times I must have been taken advantage of because I did not know how to negotiate and deal with conflict effectively. It makes me happy that I learned how to do this now, but also frustrated that I missed so many opportunities." It is hard to say it better than my former student; that short, but powerful statement, effectively articulated the value of knowing how to negotiate in life.

FURTHER READING

Fisher, Roger and Alan Sharp. *Getting It Done: How to Lead When You Are Not in Charge.* New York: Harper Collins, 1998.

Fisher, Roger and William Ury. *Getting to YES: Negotiating Agreement Without Giving In.* New York: Penguin Books, 1981.

Hall, Lavinia. *Negotiation: Strategies for Mutual Gain.* Newbury Park: Sage Press, 1993.

Lax, David and James K. Sebenius. *3-D Negotiation: Powerful Tools to Change the Game in Your Most Important Deals.* Cambridge: Harvard Business School Press, 2006.

Ury, William. *Getting Past No: Negotiating in Difficult Situations.* New York: Bantam Books, 1993.

Ury, William. *Getting to YES: Negotiating Agreement Without Giving In.* New York: Penguin Books, 1981.

NEXT STEPS IN DEVELOPING THE NEGOTIATOR IN YOU

THIS BOOK HAS PURPOSELY sought to briefly cover a wide range of topics in the various realms of negotiation. Through common day negotiation scenarios I have aimed to provide you with some thoughts on how to approach negotiations differently. In the process, skills and tactics have been embedded to help you with the how of actually negotiating these situations. And the personalization worksheets are designed for you to utilize as you close the book and take your place at the negotiating table in whatever form it takes.

Negotiation is a difficult process challenging all of our senses, from the logical to the emotional and everywhere in between. Having worked your way through this book you now have some new ideas on how to approach negotiations so that you give yourself the best chance of meeting your interests in any given situation. Much of the challenge of successful negotiation is knowledge based. However, an equally important challenge to negotiation is the level of confidence with which someone goes about the process. In one of the training sessions I recently completed, a participant summarized the essence of what I hoped to convey that day. He stated, "You taught me some new ways of looking at the negotiation process—paradigms I had never looked through before. But perhaps more importantly, I feel far more confident going into negotiations now. My apprehension has been transformed into confidence. A process I really loathed is now one that I welcome as a new and continual challenge."

The Negotiator in You has given you some breath from which to go into your future negotiations at work, at home, and in life. It is my sincere hope that you will take this book as a jumping off point and go into further depth on the subject of negotiation. There is an entire world of negotiation out there to explore and to learn from as the further reading sections of this book suggest.

Finally, remember that practice makes perfect. Negotiation is inherently a strategic endeavor that is filled with trial and error and many learning opportunities. Just when you think you have figured out the negotiation process something unexpected will happen to remind you how much there is left to learn.

A NOTE ABOUT THE AUTHOR

Dr. Joshua N. Weiss is the Co-Founder of the Global Negotiation Initiative at Harvard University. He received his Ph.D. from the Institute for Conflict Analysis and Resolution at George Mason University in 2002. Weiss has published extensively on negotiation and is an internationally recognized speaker and trainer on negotiation at the organizational, corporate, government, and international levels. He lives in East Longmeadow, Massachusetts.